WILDFLOWERS OF THE INLAND NORTHWEST

WILDFLOWERS OF THE INLAND NORTHWEST

Idaho, Montana, Washington, Oregon, British Columbia & Alberta

SIMPLIFIED IDENTIFICATION OF
216 WILDFLOWERS
FOR THE FLOWER LOVER

Interesting Comments
Both Factual and Mythical

By
Ralph and Peggy Faust

Published by
Museum of North Idaho
P.O. Box 812
Coeur d'Alene, Idaho 83814
(208) 664-3448
museumni@nidlink.com

ISBN: 0-9643647-6-X

Book editing, design, and production by
PageWorksInk
Coeur d'Alene, Idaho

Cover photograph of Indian Paint Brush by Ralph Faust
Photographs in this book are by Ralph and Peggy Faust
except for photographs of the Queen's Cup and Trumpet Lungwort provided by Penny Stritch.

Printed in Hong Kong
by Mantec Production Co.

DEDICATION

This book is dedicated to the memory of Ralph M. Faust, 1916-1997,
my friend and husband for 54 years.
He was a man of many talents,
and the photographer of most of the flowers shown in this book.
—Peggy Faust

TABLE OF CONTENTS

FOREWORD

People do some things just because they enjoy doing them. Finding, identifying and enjoying wildflowers certainly fall into this category. People do other things because they feel there is an urgent need to do them, and that is the reason for this book.

When we retired, we left mid-America to join several of our children in the West. There we began to roam the meadows, forests and mountains with our grandchildren to look for wildflowers. We found many, but identifying them was another matter.

In some wildflower books, flowers are grouped according to their "family", which is meaningless to amateurs, or are keyed scientifically in a system best understood by botanists. Even in the books which purport to simplify identification, the flower descriptions rely on terms such as "ovaries", "tubular calyx", and "stipules". This does not make identification impossible, but it does necessitate additional work and more patience. Further, in many of the books only a portion of the pictures is in color, while the remainder is merely black and white sketches. The result is that many people have difficulty with flower identification.

We have attempted to resolve these problems by including in a single volume 216 wildflowers commonly found in the Inland Northwest region, all with full-color photographs, organized in a manner which makes them easy for ordinary non-technical wildflower lovers to identify.

ACKNOWLEDGEMENTS

When we began this book, we knew little about wildflowers except that we liked them. Writing the book was an enjoyable learning experience, which required the help and expertise of other people.

We thank master gardener Patsy Molinare for her help at the very beginning of our project, and librarian Jean Clark for locating the many books we needed for study and identification.

We are especially grateful to botanist Jill Blake, formerly with the U.S. Forest Service, and to LeAnn Eno, botanist, Bureau of Land Management, Coeur d'Alene District, for their help with identification of species and for many other suggestions.

We also thank Penny Stritch for providing photographs of the Queen's Cup and Trumpet Lungwort. And, finally, we thank our sons Peter, for the use of his computer, Vincent, David, Stephen, and Jerry for their time and technical expertise; all our family and friends for their continual encouragement; and all who made Ralph's dream of publishing this book a reality.

HOW TO USE THIS BOOK

Using our book is simplicity itself. It requires no technical knowledge regarding plants or flowers, but relies on two prominent features: the color and the number of petals. Therefore, to find a particular flower in this book, you will first turn to the proper color section, selecting from white, yellow, orange, red-pink, lavender-purple, blue or brown. You will next refer to the number of petals and, finally, to the photographs.

While color is the dominant characteristic of a flower, it is not always totally reliable. There are certain flowers which occur in several colors, or in a color other than that which the name suggests. For example, Phlox, which may be white, pink, lavender, or blue, is shown here with the white flowers. Blue-Eyed Grass, which we include with the blue flowers, shades from white to blue and to pink, lavender, and purple.

To help overcome this problem, we have included at the beginning of each color section a list of the flowers which may occur in colors other than that of the section in which they are shown. For example, if you find a five-petalled blue flower and cannot find it in the blue flower section, look in other color sections for five-petalled flowers which have the same appearance. If you believe you may have identified it, refer to the list mentioned above to check if it also occurs in the color you found. Basically, however, you will go from the color to the number of petals, and then to the pictures. Where the diameter of the flower head might be of interest or may be a factor in identification, the average diameter is given.

COMMENTS

While these comments do not affect our system of flower identification, they are included for those interested in strict accuracy of definitions.

There are some flowers, such as the Toad Flax and the Clematis, which have no true petals, but which have petal-like sepals which to the casual viewer appear to be petals. There are other flowers, such as Blue-eyed Grass, which have sepals and petals that look alike. For purposes of identification in both of these instances, we have counted the number of sepals and considered them to be petals.

Furthermore there are plants, such as the Sunflower, having both disc flowers and ray flowers, giving the overall appearance to the casual observer of a single flower with many petals. So we have taken the liberty of including such flowers in the "many petals" category.

Wildflowers wherein the individual blossoms form a raceme or a spike are so distinctive in appearance that we have placed them in a separate classification (raceme) regardless of the number of petals in each flower head. Beargrass, Lupines, and Mulleins are good examples of such flowers.

We also list a flowering season. This does not mean that a particular flower will bloom in one particular area for the duration of the stated period. If the season is said to be June to August, you may find the flowers blooming in one area in June, in a drier area in July, and perhaps at a higher elevation in late July and August. We have found Buttercups in each of the twelve months of the year.

Also included are a glossary of terms referring to flower parts, an index of common names and of scientific names, as well as interesting facts, and in some cases myths, regarding names, derivation of names, leaf structure, edibility, possible uses, et cetera, as applicable to each flower.

While we mention traditional lore with regard to edibility, we do not recommend eating any plants. No part of any plant should be eaten by anyone who is not certain it will cause no ill effects.

GLOSSARY

ANTHER .... The part of the stamen which contains the pollen.
AXIL .... The upper angle formed by a leaf with the stem.
BASAL .... At the base of the flower.
BRACT .... A tiny leaf on the stem near the base of a flower.
CALYX .... The outer circle of flower parts, made up of sepals which are behind and usually smaller than the flower petals.
COMPOSITE .... Made up of a disk of many small flowers, usually surrounded by a plurality of ray flowers.
CORM .... The enlarged base of an underground stem.
COROLLA .... The inner circle of flowering parts, made up of the flower's petals.
CORYMB .... A flat-topped or oval-topped flower cluster with stems arising from different levels on the main stem.
DISK .... The central flowers of a composite. Also called a diskflower.
HERB .... A plant whose stems die back to the ground after each season's growth.
INVOLUCRE .... Bracts surrounding a flower or flower cluster.
LANCEOLATE .... Lance-shaped.
LEAFLET .... One of the small blades of a compound leaf.
LINEAR .... Long and very narrow and having parallel edges.
OVATE .... Having the shape of an egg.
PISTIL .... The central organ of a flower consisting of an ovary, a style and a stigma. The pistil produces seeds.
RACEME .... An elongated flower cluster along a single stalk, the flowers having stems and being youngest at the top.
RAY .... The elongated extensions of the corolla of a composite. For example, the outer "petals" of a daisy.
ROSETTE .... A circular cluster of leaves, usually at the base of a plant.
SEPAL .... An individual segment of the calyx.
SERRATED .... Saw-toothed.
SPATHE .... A large bract enclosing a flower cluster, as in Skunk Cabbage.
SPIKE .... An elongated flower cluster with stalkless or nearly stalkless flowers.
STAMEN .... The male organ of a flower, usually surrounding the pistil and comprising a stemlike filament and a tip, called the anther, which carries pollen.
STIGMA .... The terminal part of a pistil that receives pollen.
STYLE .... The part of the pistil between the ovary and the stigma.
UMBEL .... A roughly flat-topped flower cluster having all the stalks arising from the same point.

ABOUT THE AUTHORS

Ralph and Peggy Faust lived in North Idaho for many years, where they were faithful members of the Calypso Chapter of the Idaho Native Plant Society. They wrote this book together and collected the photographs over years of happy hiking.

Ralph, unfortunately, did not live to see the book in print. Peggy has fulfilled their dream with the assistance of the Museum of North Idaho, especially the members of the book committee.

Ralph Faust held a B.S. in Mechanical Engineering from the Illinois Institute of Technology and a law degree from Chicago-Kent School of Law, with postdoctoral studies in patent law. Peggy Faust holds a bachelor of arts from Mundelein College, Chicago, and a teaching certificate. Together they raised ten children.

WHITE	OTHER POSSIBLE COLORS
Aster	lavender, blue
Avalanche Lily	yellow
Blue-eyed Grass	pink, lavender, purple, blue
Buckbrush	lavender, blue
Fairy Bell	greenish yellow
Fawn Lily	yellow
Fleabane	pink, lavender
Field Mint	lavender
Foxglove	yellow, lavender
Groundsel	yellow
Honeysuckle	yellow, orange, red
Indian Paint Brush	yellow, orange, red
Kinnikinnick	pink
Lady's Slipper	yellow, pink
Larkspur	pink, purple, blue
Mariposa	yellow, lavender
Miner's Lettuce	pink
Parrot's Beak	yellow, pink, lavender
Penstemon	red, lavender, blue
Phlox	pink, lavender, blue
Pinedrops	red, pink
Siberian Lettuce	pink
Skullcap	pink, blue
Spring Beauty	pink
Trillium	red, purple
Twisted Stalk	greenish white
Violet	yellow, red, purple, blue
Wild Clover	pink, red
Wild Hyacinth	blue
Wild Sweet Pea	pink, lavender
Wood Sorrel	yellow, lavender

ARROWHEAD

Arrowhead Family
Sagittaria latifolia

WHERE FOUND:
Shallow water of ponds and lakes.

FLOWERING SEASON:
July to September

COMMENTS: (2")
The Indians called this plant "wapato". The flower pictured is the broad-leaved variety. Note the tiny white flower and the huge arrow-shaped leaves. Other species have ovate or grasslike leaves. The underground tubers were roasted and eaten by both Indians and early settlers.

BIG POD MARIPOSA

Lily Family
Calochortus eurycarpus

WHERE FOUND:
Well drained soil of meadows and woods.

FLOWERING SEASON:
June to July.

COMMENTS: (2")
A green band separates a yellow area at the base of each petal from a squarish purple mark in the petal's center. The Sego Lily, *C. nuttallii*, the state flower of Utah, has a large crescent-shaped mark directly above the yellow basal area.

LADY'S SLIPPER

Orchid Family
Cypripedium montanum

WHERE FOUND:
Open to wooded mountain habitats.

FLOWERING SEASON:
May to August.

COMMENTS:
This flower is also called the Mountain Lady Slipper. *Cypripedium* means Venus's slipper, from the Greek *Kypris*, for Venus, and *podion,* for slipper. The Showy Lady's Slipper, a pink variety, is the state flower of Minnesota. There is also a yellow variety.

MARIPOSA

Lily Family
Calochortus apiculatus

WHERE FOUND:
High, sunny, open rocky areas.

FLOWERING SEASON:
June to July.

COMMENTS: (1¾")
There are several species of Mariposas, all having more or less hairy petals. Mariposas may be creamy white, yellow or lavender. Mariposa is the Spanish word for butterfly, and the markings on Mariposa petals often resemble the colored wings of some butterflies.

ARROWHEAD

BIG POD MARIPOSA

LADY'S SLIPPER

MARIPOSA

WESTERN TRILLIUM

BITTERCRESS

BUNCHBERRY

WESTERN TRILLIUM

Lily Family
Trillium ovatum

WHERE FOUND:
Moist shaded areas.

FLOWERING SEASON:
March to June.

COMMENTS: (1" to 3")
There are some dozen species of Trillium but, as the name implies, all are distinguished by their major parts being in threes—three leaflets, three sepals and three petals. The petals of some species are red to reddish purple, but even the petals of the white species turn pink after the flower is fertilized, and with age. The species pictured is sometimes called the Wake Robin, symbolizing early spring. However, in some areas, a red variety is called Wake Robin, so we can't trust too much in common names.

BITTERCRESS

Mustard Family
Cardamine Sp.

WHERE FOUND:
Moist woods and stream banks.

FLOWERING SEASON:
April to August.

COMMENTS: (¼")
There are several species of Bittercress. Young leaves may be used in salads, and they have a sharper taste than Watercress. Bittercress is sometimes confused with Watercress, but the latter tends to be a prostrate, floating plant, whereas Bittercress stands erect.

BUNCHBERRY

Dogwood Family
Cornus canadensis

WHERE FOUND:
Moist, shady slopes of meadows and woods, up to 8000 feet.

FLOWERING SEASON:
May to July.

COMMENTS: (1 ½")
Bunchberry, also known as Canadian Dogwood, develops bright red berries. What appear to be four white petals are really bracts surrounding many tiny yellowish flowers. The fresh berries were eaten by the Indians, while the leaves are a favored food of white-tailed deer.

FENDLER'S PENNY GRASS

Mustard Family
Thlaspi fendleri

WHERE FOUND:
Moist rocky areas.

FLOWERING SEASON:
May to August.

COMMENTS: (3/16")
The members of this family are herbs. The family name, *Cruciferae,* means crucifix, and refers to the four petals in the form of a cross.

HOARY CRESS

Mustard Family
Cardaria draba

WHERE FOUND:
Open fields and roadsides.

FLOWERING SEASON:
April to July.

COMMENTS: (3/16")
This flower is also called the Heart-podded Hoarycress or Whitetop. The flowers grow from an underground series of runners.

PENNYCRESS

Mustard Family
Thlaspi arvens

WHERE FOUND:
Open fields and roadsides.

FLOWERING SEASON:
May to August.

COMMENTS: (¼")
The name is derived from the deeply notched round pods, extending along the stem, which are the shape and approximate size of a penny. The plant is also called Fanweed.

SYRINGA

Hydrangeaceae Family
Philadelphus lewisii

WHERE FOUND:
Open fields, meadows and roadsides up to 7000 feet.

FLOWERING SEASON:
May to July.

COMMENTS: (1")
The Syringa is the state flower of Idaho. It blossoms on a shrub which is also known as Mock Orange. The Indians of the Northwest used the straight stems of the shrub to make arrows.

FENDLER'S PENNY GRASS

HOARY CRESS

PENNYCRESS

SYRINGA

WHITLOW GRASS

WILD LILY-OF-THE-VALLEY

BIRCHLEAF SPIREA

BLUE-EYED MARY

WHITLOW GRASS

Mustard Family
Draba verna

WHERE FOUND:
Dry to sandy meadows.

FLOWERING SEASON:
March to May.

COMMENTS: (3/8")
There are some half-dozen species growing from low to high elevations in the mountains. Note the very deeply cleft petals and the alternate flat pods projecting from the stems. There is a basal cluster of elliptical leaves.

WILD LILY-OF-THE-VALLEY

Lily Family
Maianthemum canadense

WHERE FOUND:
Moist areas of valleys and mountains.

FLOWERING SEASON:
May to July.

COMMENTS: (3/16")
This flower is also called Canada Mayflower. It is similar to False Solomon's Seal, except that it has single flowers on branching stems. Both the shoots and leaves are edible. This flower is an exception in the Lily family, in that its parts are in fours rather than in threes or sixes.

WHITE 5 PETALS

BIRCHLEAF SPIREA

Rose Family
Spiraea betulifolia

WHERE FOUND:
Moist to dry open woods and along streams.

FLOWERING SEASON:
June to August.

COMMENTS: (¼")
Also called Meadow Sweet. Several species occur in the Western conifer forests. The 1"- 2" coarsely toothed oval leaves are glossy green above. Grouse eat the leaves in spring, and deer browse on the shrub in summer.

BLUE-EYED MARY

Figwort Family
Collinsia parviflora

WHERE FOUND:
Moist meadows and woods.

FLOWERING SEASON:
April to June.

COMMENTS: (¼")
In this flower, the upper two petals are white, the lower two are blue. There is a fifth petal, in the center of the lower lip, folded over the pollen-bearing stamen.

BUCKBRUSH

Buckthorn Family
Ceanothus sanguineus

WHERE FOUND:
Dry mountain slopes, open areas, frequently under pine stands.

FLOWERING SEASON:
June to September.

COMMENTS:
The flowers may be white, lavender or blue, and are sometimes called Snowbrush. The 1–2" broad, finely toothed oval leaves are dark green above and very light beneath. It is said that some Indian tribes used the leaves for tobacco. Big game love to browse it.

CASCADE AZALEA

Rhododendron Family
Rhododendron albiflorum

WHERE FOUND:
Moist places at higher altitudes.

FLOWERING SEASON:
June to August.

COMMENTS: (¾")
The flowers of this shrub grow in clusters of two or three. They have a mild citrus odor.

CHICKWEED

Pink Family
Cerastium arvense

WHERE FOUND:
Dry open fields and sandy areas at all elevations.

FLOWERING SEASON:
April to September.

COMMENTS: (¾")
There are numerous species of Chickweed. The pictured Field Chickweed is rangier than most others. Though it is a troublesome weed, both stems and leaves may be eaten either raw or boiled.

COW PARSNIP

Parsley Family
Heracleum lanatum

WHERE FOUND:
Meadows, open woods, along streams.

FLOWERING SEASON:
May to August.

COMMENTS:
The plant, also called Hogweed, has an unpleasant odor. The umbel of flowers can be up to 12 inches across. The plant is a good forage crop. However, the juice and hairs of the stem can irritate the skin.

BUCKBRUSH

CASCADE AZALEA

CHICKWEED

COW PARSNIP

ELDERBERRY

CRYPTANTHA

FALSE MITERWORT

GREENLEAF MANZANITA

CRYPTANTHA

Borage Family
Cryptantha torreyana

WHERE FOUND:
Dry, sunny areas.

FLOWERING SEASON:
May to July.

COMMENTS: (1/3")
The flower name comes from *cryptos* for hidden and *anthos* for flower, because the first discovered species had very small flowers. As a matter of fact, most of the species are very difficult to tell apart.

ELDERBERRY

Honeysuckle Family
Sambucus racemosa

WHERE FOUND:
Damp soil in open areas.

FLOWERING SEASON:
June to August.

COMMENTS:
This species has white to cream-colored flower clusters and produces the delicious blue berries that pickers seek for pies and jelly. The 5"- 7" opposite lance-shaped leaves are sharply toothed.

FALSE MITERWORT

Grossulariaceae Family
Tiarella trifoliata var. laciniata

WHERE FOUND:
Moist shady woods and stream banks.

FLOWERING SEASON:
May to August.

COMMENTS: (¼")
Sometimes called Foamflower. The genus name *Tiarella* comes from the Greek word *tiara*, for an ancient Persian headdress which the fruit of this flower resembles.

GREENLEAF MANZANITA

Heath Family
Arctostaphylos patula

WHERE FOUND:
Open conifer forests.

FLOWERING SEASON:
May to July.

COMMENTS:
The name *manzanita* means "little apple" in Spanish. The plant regenerates rapidly after a fire. The fruit is eaten by birds, bears and small mammals. Deer browse on the leaves.

HIMALAYAN BLACKBERRY

Rose Family
Rubus discolor (procerus)

WHERE FOUND:
Roadsides and open areas.

FLOWERING SEASON:
June to August.

COMMENTS:
This shrub was transported to the United States from Europe. It forms dense bramble patches which furnish both food and refuge for wildlife.

INDIAN PIPE

Heath Family
Monotropa uniflora

WHERE FOUND:
Moist shaded woods.

FLOWERING SEASON:
May to July.

COMMENTS: (½")
Indian Pipe contains no chlorophyll, which gives plants their green color and changes light energy into chemical energy, or "food" for the plant. Indian Pipe is a saprophyte—a plant which lives on dead or decaying fungi or other plant matter. It turns black with age or when picked.

KINNIKINNICK

Heath Family
Arctostaphylos uva-ursi

WHERE FOUND:
Rich soil in open woods.

FLOWERING SEASON:
March to June.

COMMENTS: (¼")
Kinnikinnick, also called Bearberry, is a low-lying shrub whose name is an Indian word for a tobacco substitute. Flowers may be white or pink. The leaves and twigs are eaten by deer and mountain sheep. The berries are eaten by black bear and birds, and once were eaten by Indians and Eskimos. Smoke from the leaves was inhaled as a headache remedy.

LARGE-LEAVED SANDWORT

Pink Family
Arenaria macrophylla

WHERE FOUND:
Sandy soil in shaded woodlands.

FLOWERING SEASON:
June to August.

COMMENTS: (½")
The genus name comes from the Latin word *arena*, meaning sand. This refers to the preferred soil of most species of sandworts.

HIMALAYAN BLACKBERRY

INDIAN PIPE

KINNIKINNICK AND BERRY

LARGE-LEAVED SANDWORT

MINER'S LETTUCE

MORNING GLORY

MOUNTAIN SANDWORT

NINEBARK

MINER'S LETTUCE

Purslane Family
Montia perfoliata

WHERE FOUND:
Streambanks and moist open woodlands and meadows.

FLOWERING SEASON:
May to July.

COMMENTS: (3/8")
The stem passes through the center of what appears to be a round leaf but which is two leaves grown together. Most of these flowers grow only 3 to 6 inches tall, and may be white or pink. The leaves are edible.

MORNING GLORY

Morning Glory Family
Convolvulus arvensis

WHERE FOUND:
Fields, roadsides and waste places.

FLOWERING SEASON:
May to August.

COMMENTS: (1")
The Morning Glory is a low-lying plant which spreads to form dense patches that might cover acres. Also known as Bindweed, it causes very serious problems for farmers.

MOUNTAIN SANDWORT

Pink Family
Arenaria capillaris

WHERE FOUND:
Sunny rocky areas.

FLOWERING SEASON:
June to July.

COMMENTS: (3/8")
This flower has also been called Beautiful Sandwort. There are more than 150 species of Arenaria. The genus name comes from the Latin word *arena*, meaning sand. *Arenaria* means sand-loving.

NINEBARK

Rose Family
Physocarpus malvaceus

WHERE FOUND:
Sunny open hillsides.

FLOWERING SEASON:
June to July.

COMMENTS:
Ninebark has many layers of shreddy bark. It was once thought to have precisely nine layers.

OCEAN SPRAY

Rose Family
Holodiscus discolor

WHERE FOUND:
Woodlands and disturbed areas.

FLOWERING SEASON:
May to August.

COMMENTS:
Also known as Cream Bush. The leaves are alternate, ovate, and coarsely toothed. The flowers grow in dense clusters, making it a beautiful ornamental. The Indians made arrows from the straight branches.

PARROT'S BEAK

Figwort Family
Pedicularis racemosa

WHERE FOUND:
Moist shaded to open areas.

FLOWERING SEASON:
June to September.

COMMENTS: (5/8")
Parrot's Beak is sometimes called Lousewort. *P. groenlandica* may be pink or lavender, while *P. canadensis* is yellow. It was once believed that livestock feeding on these plants became infested with lice.

POKER ALUMROOT

Saxifrage Family
Heuchera cylindrica

WHERE FOUND:
Rocky slopes and woodlands.

FLOWERING SEASON:
April to August.

COMMENTS: (3/8")
Flowers tend from white to a greenish cream. Leaves are lobed and maple-like. The genus was named after a German botanist named Heucher. Indians boiled the roots with Sumac blossoms to make a medicine used for teething. Roots were also used to treat indigestion.

PRINCE'S PINE

Wintergreen Family
Chimaphila umbellata

WHERE FOUND:
Coniferous woods and rocky areas.

FLOWERING SEASON:
May to September.

COMMENTS: (½")
Prince's Pine is also called Pipsissewa, a name believed to be derived from the Cree, meaning "it breaks into small pieces". The Cree were referring to the juice of the plant breaking up kidney stones or gallstones. It was once used in medicine for eyedrops. Prince's Pine is beautiful from front and back and reminds one of a miniature birthday cake.

OCEAN SPRAY

⮝ PARROT'S BEAK

⮝ POKER ALUMROOT

PRINCE'S PINE
FRONT AND BACK ⮞

SCORCHED PENSTEMON

SERVICEBERRY

SIBERIAN LETTUCE

SILVERLEAF PHACELIA

SCORCHED PENSTEMON

Snapdragon Family
Penstemon deustus

WHERE FOUND:
Dry, rocky areas.

FLOWERING SEASON:
May to June.

COMMENTS: (1 ½")
This is the only white flowered penstemon. Other varieties may be red, lavender or blue. The word penstemon was originally written pentstemon, meaning 5 stamen. Because one of the stamen is bearded, the Penstemon is also called Beardtongue. Note the notched leaves.

SERVICEBERRY

Rose Family
Amelanchier alnifolia

WHERE FOUND:
Drier soils of woods and fields.

FLOWERING SEASON:
April to June

COMMENTS: (1")
Both the dark blue berries and the leaves are eaten by animals. The berries are also eaten by humans or made into jelly or wine. The Indians made pemmican by pounding the berries and buffalo meat into cakes and allowing the cakes to dry.

SIBERIAN LETTUCE

Purslane Family
Montia cordifolia

WHERE FOUND:
Moist open areas.

FLOWERING SEASON:
May to July.

COMMENTS: (½")
Flowers may be white or pink. Siberian Lettuce is related to Miner's Lettuce, except that the flower rises between a distinct pair of opposed leaves. It is also called Heartleaf Montia and Siberian Candyflower.

SILVERLEAF PHACELIA

Waterleaf Family
Phacelia hastata

WHERE FOUND:
Dry, rocky, disturbed areas.

FLOWERING SEASON:
May to July.

COMMENTS:
Note that the flowers bud only on one side of a coiled stem. Some twenty species occur in the Inland Northwest. Some species are grazed by deer and elk.

SPRING BEAUTY

Purslane Family
Claytonia lanceolata

WHERE FOUND:
Moist soils, low to high altitudes.

FLOWERING SEASON:
April to July.

COMMENTS: (1")
The Spring Beauty has just a single pair of opposed leaves. The flowers may be white or pink but the petals always have dark pink veins. The flower grows from a spherical corm that is edible and, when cooked, tastes something like potatoes.

STICKY CURRANT

Gooseberry Family
Ribes viscosissimum

WHERE FOUND:
Sunny slopes.

FLOWERING SEASON:
May to June.

COMMENTS:
The leaves and flowers are sticky. Twigs and leaves are also hairy. The berries are blue-black, sticky and not edible. The genus *Ribes* includes both currants and gooseberries, which, of course, are edible.

SUGAR SCOOP

Grossulariaceae Family
Tiarella trifoliata var. unifoliata

WHERE FOUND:
Shady moist woods.

FLOWERING SEASON:
May to August.

COMMENTS: (¼")
This is the single Sugar Scoop, having single maple-like leaves. The triple Sugar Scoop, *T. trifoliata*, not shown, has each leaf divided into three distinct leaflets.

SUNDEW

Sundew Family
Drosera rotundifolia

WHERE FOUND:
Sphagnum bogs.

FLOWERING SEASON:
July to September.

COMMENTS:
The eye-catching feature of the plant is the small basal ring of round red leaves with red hairs. The leaves exude a sticky fluid which attracts and traps insects. A cluster of small white flowers rises on a slender stem from the center of the basal ring.

SPRING BEAUTY

STICKY CURRANT

SUGAR SCOOP

SUNDEW

THIMBLEBERRY

VIBURNUM ➢

WILD STRAWBERRY

WINDFLOWER ➢

THIMBLEBERRY

Rose Family
Rubus parviflorus

WHERE FOUND:
Near streams and in moist to dry areas of open forests.

FLOWERING SEASON:
April to July.

COMMENTS: (1½")
The Thimbleberry is sometimes called the White Flowered Raspberry. In fact, it is related to both the raspberry and the blackberry. The fruit is edible and sweet and is an important seasonal food for both mammals and birds.

VIBURNUM

Honeysuckle Family
Viburnum ellipticum

WHERE FOUND:
Open woods.

FLOWERING SEASON:
May to June.

COMMENTS:
There are over one hundred species worldwide, but only about fifteen in the United States. Both birds and mammals eat the tart berries.

WILD STRAWBERRY

Rose Family
Fragaria vesca

WHERE FOUND:
Moist soil in woods, meadows and along streams

FLOWERING SEASON:
May to August.

COMMENTS: (1")
The berries are small, but sweet. The leaves can be used for tea. The name Strawberry comes from the custom of laying straw around the plants for protection against the weather.

WINDFLOWER

Buttercup Family
Anemone piperi

WHERE FOUND:
Moist woods and meadows.

FLOWERING SEASON:
April to June.

COMMENTS:
According to the writer Pliny, these flowers could only open at the bidding of the wind. Hence they were called Windflowers, from the Greek word *anemos*, meaning wind. The plant is also called Piper's Anemone.

WOODLAND STAR

WHERE FOUND:
Shaded woodlands.

FLOWERING SEASON:
March to June.

Saxifrage Family
Lithophragma parviflora

COMMENTS: (¾")
There are more than twelve species in western North America. The rootstocks have tiny bulblets which are eaten by rodents. The leaves are basal and deeply divided.

YARROW

WHERE FOUND:
Open dry meadows and disturbed areas.

FLOWERING SEASON:
May to October.

Composite Family
Achillea millefolium

COMMENTS: (¼")
Yarrow contains a chemical which promotes blood clotting. This gave rise to such names as Bloodwort, Nosebleed and Woundwort. *Achillea* derives from the legend that the centaur Chiron advised the Greek hero Achilles to use the plant to staunch the wounds of his soldiers during the siege of Troy. Indians made a decoction from the leaves and inhaled its vapors for headaches.

WHITE 6 PETALS

DEATH CAMAS

WHERE FOUND:
Open areas.

FLOWERING SEASON:
May to July.

Lily Family
Zigadenus venenosus

COMMENTS: (½")
Deadly poisonous alkaloids are concentrated in the bulb. Death Camas sometimes grows near the edible blue-petaled Camas and the leaves of both varieties are grasslike, so bulbs should not be collected when the plants are not in bloom.

FAIRYBELL

WHERE FOUND:
Moist shaded woods.

FLOWERING SEASON:
May to July.

Lily Family
Disporum trachycarpum

COMMENTS: (¾")
Flowers may be white to pale greenish-yellow and grow at the tips of branched stems. There is a difference of opinion as to whether the orange-red berries are edible. The consensus of opinion calls them tasty and edible. A novice should always be certain of edibility before eating any plant.

WOODLAND STAR

YARROW

∢ DEATH CAMAS

FAIRYBELL AND BERRY

FAWN LILY

⮝ GOLDTHREAD
IN SEED ⮟

PRICKLY POPPY

QUEEN'S CUP ➤

FAWN LILY

WHERE FOUND:
Subalpine meadows and forests.

FLOWERING SEASON:
March to August.

Lily Family
Erythronium grandiflorum var. candidum

COMMENTS: (2½")
The flowers are nodding, with the petals and sepals strongly turned backward. All parts of the plant are edible and bears feed on them in spring. *Var. candidum* is also known as the Avalanche Lily.

GOLDTHREAD

WHERE FOUND:
Cool moist woods in mountains and foothills.

FLOWERING SEASON:
March to May.

Buttercup Family
Coptis occidentalis

COMMENTS: (¾")
The plant is named for its threadlike golden yellow roots. The roots are astringent and were once used as a yellow dye and as a tonic. The flower petals drop very soon after blossoming, so you are more likely to see the seed pods as shown.

PRICKLY POPPY

WHERE FOUND:
Dry disturbed areas.

FLOWERING SEASON:
June to July.

Poppy Family
Papaver argemone

COMMENTS:
Most members of the Poppy family have four petals, but the Prickly Poppy usually has six.

QUEEN'S CUP

WHERE FOUND:
Moist coniferous woods.

FLOWERING SEASON:
May to July.

Lily Family
Clintonia uniflora

COMMENTS: (1")
The flower is also called Bride's Bonnet. The plant has two to five lance-shaped leaves, and spreads from an extensive system of underground stems. The fruit is a lustrous deep blue berry. Clintonia was named for DeWitt Clinton, an early governor of New York as well as a naturalist.

STARRY SOLOMON'S SEAL

Lily Family
Smilacina stellata

WHERE FOUND:
Moist woods.

FLOWERING SEASON:
March to June.

COMMENTS: (¼")
This flower is similar to False Solomon's Seal, *S. racemosa,* except that each flower bud is on a separate stalk. The berries are edible in small quantities.

TWISTED STALK

Lily Family
Streptopus amplexifolius

WHERE FOUND:
Moist woods and along streams.

FLOWERING SEASON:
May to July.

COMMENTS: (½")
Also called White Mandarin because the blossoms resemble chinese lanterns. The blossoms may be off-white to pale green. The hidden flowers are borne in the leaf axils on slender stalks having a distinct twist, hence the name.

WHITE MANY PETALS

BANEBERRY

Buttercup Family
Actaea rubra

WHERE FOUND:
Shaded woods and stream banks.

FLOWERING SEASON:
May to July.

COMMENTS:
This species is often called Western Baneberry. The glassy berries may be dark red or white, and both the berries and the roots are poisonous. The sepals and petals drop almost immediately, leaving the many white stamen which we perceive as petals.

COTTON GRASS

Sedge Family
Eriophorum polystachion

WHERE FOUND:
Bogs and meadows up to 9000 feet.

FLOWERING SEASON:
June to July.

COMMENTS:
There are about twenty species of Cotton Grass, sometimes called Cotton Sedge. The leaves are grasslike. Silky hairs project from inconspicuous flowers.

STARRY SOLOMON'S SEAL

TWISTED STALK

⮝ BANEBERRY ⮞

COTTON GRASS

ENGELMANN ASTER

FALSE BUGBANE

FLEABANE

MAYWEED

ENGELMANN ASTER

Composite Family
Aster engelmannii

WHERE FOUND:
Moist woods and open areas.

FLOWERING SEASON:
June to September.

COMMENTS: (2")
Asters provide browse for big game animals. The long, lance-shaped leaves were boiled and eaten by western Indians. Asters are often confused with Daisies, but Asters are usually larger and have three or more overlapping layers of green bracts around the flower head.

FALSE BUGBANE

Buttercup Family
Trautvetteria caroliniensis

WHERE FOUND:
Moist woods.

FLOWERING SEASON:
May to August.

COMMENTS:
False Bugbane has no petals, but is recognized by its numerous white stamen. It is distinguished from Bugbane and Baneberry by its large, deeply cleft, maple-like leaves.

FLEABANE

Composite Family
Erigeron compositus

WHERE FOUND:
Dry sandy soils and along roadsides.

FLOWERING SEASON:
March to October.

COMMENTS: (¾")
Also called the Cutleaf Daisy. The rays of Fleabanes may be white, pink, or lavender, but the center or disk is always yellow. Each stem ends in a single flower head. The leaves are mostly basal and deeply notched. It was once thought that the flower repelled fleas, hence the name. Note the numerous, narrow rays of equal length, distinguishing the Fleabanes from the Field Daisies with their fewer, petal-like rays.

MAYWEED

Composite Family
Anthemis cotula

WHERE FOUND:
Roadsides and prairies.

FLOWERING SEASON:
June to October.

COMMENTS: (1")
This flower is also called Dog Fennel. Look for slightly conical disk flowers and notched, lacy leaves which have an acrid taste and a disagreeable odor. If handled they may produce blisters.

OXEYE DAISY

Composite Family
Chrysanthemum leucanthemum

WHERE FOUND:
Open prairies and fields.

FLOWERING SEASON:
May to October.

COMMENTS: (2")
Also called Field Daisy. Look for a yellow disk with a "dimple" in the center. The flower is a pesky weed, difficult to eradicate. The name Daisy is said to come from "day's eye" because the flowers close at night. Note the petal-like quality of the rays, distinguishing these Daisies from the Fleabanes.

PEARLY EVERLASTING

Composite Family
Anaphalis margaritacea

WHERE FOUND:
Coniferous forests, roadcuts and other disturbed areas.

FLOWERING SEASON:
June to September.

COMMENTS: ($^{3}/_{8}$")
There are about 25 species of *Anaphalis*. The flowers dry beautifully for flower arrangements. *Margaritacea* means pearly. The flower has also been called Indian Tobacco.

WATER LILY

Water Lily Family
Nymphaea odorata

WHERE FOUND:
Shallow lakes and ponds.

FLOWERING SEASON:
June to August.

COMMENTS:
The flowers have a pleasant odor. They open in the morning and close by late afternoon. The round floating leaves may be ten inches across.

WHITE WESTERN GROUNDSEL

Composite Family
Senecio integerrimus var. ochroleucus

WHERE FOUND:
Dry open woods up to the timber line.

FLOWERING SEASON:
May to August.

COMMENTS:
S. integerrimus is a yellow variety called Tower Butterweed. *Var. ochroleucus* is the only white Groundsel we have seen.

OXEYE DAISY

PEARLY EVERLASTING

WATER LILY

WHITE WESTERN GROUNDSEL

BEAR GRASS

BOG ORCHID

CHOKE CHERRY

⮝ DEVIL'S CLUB
BERRIES ⮞

BEAR GRASS

Lily Family
Xerophyllum tenax

WHERE FOUND:
Open woods and meadows.

FLOWERING SEASON:
May to August.

COMMENTS:
A graceful plant growing to five feet tall. Leaves are needle-like along the stem. The root stalks are edible if roasted. The Indians fashioned garments and baskets from the tough leaves. Each tiny flower has six petals.

BOG ORCHID

Orchid Family
Habenaria dilatata

WHERE FOUND:
Bogs and swampy areas, frequently at high elevations.

FLOWERING SEASON:
June to August.

COMMENTS:
The flowers are waxy and have a long spur. The tubers were eaten by Indians. When boiled they taste something like potatoes. The flower is also called White Bog Orchid.

CHOKE CHERRY

Rose Family
Prunus melanocarpa

WHERE FOUND:
Moist areas to 8000'.

FLOWERING SEASON:
May to June.

COMMENTS:
Also called the Black Choke Cherry. *Melanocarpa* means black-fruited. The fruit is edible, but tart. It is great for jelly or wine. The small flowers have five petals. The leaves are poisonous in spring and summer. The twigs and buds are winter browse for deer, elk, and moose. Birds eat the fruit. Indians ate the cherries fresh as well as drying them for winter use.

DEVIL'S CLUB

Ginseng Family
Oplopanax horridum

WHERE FOUND:
Streamsides and other wet areas in shady forests.

FLOWERING SEASON:
June to August.

COMMENTS:
This plant is aptly named. Not only do the stems carry sharp thorns, but the huge maple-like leaves are sharp-spined. The tiny flowers are greenish white and are followed by bright waxy red berries.

FALSE HELLEBORE

Lily Family
Veratrum californicum

WHERE FOUND:
Moist open meadows.

FLOWERING SEASON:
June to August.

COMMENTS:
This poisonous plant is also called Corn Lily. Dry powdered roots have been used as an insecticide. The species *V. viride*, also called Indian Poke, has drooping spikes and tiny greenish six-petalled flowers.

FALSE SOLOMON'S SEAL

Lily Family
Smilacina racemosa

WHERE FOUND:
Shaded woods.

FLOWERING SEASON:
April to June.

COMMENTS: (1/8")
Also called Spikenard. The berries are bitter, but juicy and edible. The stems are tipped above the leaves with elongated branched clusters of tiny white flowers. The true Solomon's Seal, which we have not found in this area, has similar leaves, but the flowers are below the leaves and grow from the leaf axils.

HOODED LADIES' TRESSES

Orchid Family
Spiranthes romanzoffiana

WHERE FOUND:
Marshes and wet meadows.

FLOWERING SEASON:
July to August.

COMMENTS:
The flowers tend to spiral in three ranks like braided hair. They are faintly scented.

PINEDROPS

Wintergreen Family
Pterospora andromedea

WHERE FOUND:
Shaded areas in coniferous forests, especially in humus under Ponderosa pines.

FLOWERING SEASON:
June to August.

COMMENTS: (3/8")
The lantern-like flowers range from white to pink to red and are carried on a thick red stalk. The genus name comes from the Greek words for "winged seeds". The plant lacks chlorophyll. The flowers have five petals.

FALSE HELLEBORE

FALSE SOLOMON'S SEAL

HOODED LADIES' TRESSES

PINEDROPS

RABBIT-FOOT CLOVER

ROUND-LEAVED REIN ORCHID

SIDE-FLOWERED MITERWORT

WHITE SWEET CLOVER

RABBIT-FOOT CLOVER

WHERE FOUND:
Roadsides and disturbed areas.

FLOWERING SEASON:
June to August.

Pea Family
Trifolium arvense

COMMENTS: (¾")
The flower heads are ½" to ¾" long. The white flowers are nearly hidden by a grayish-pinkish fuzz. As in all clovers, the roots, stems, and leaves are edible.

ROUND-LEAVED REIN ORCHID

WHERE FOUND:
Rich damp woods.

FLOWERING SEASON:
June to August.

Orchid Family
Habenaria orbiculata

COMMENTS:
The flowers have long spurs and a slender lip. The petals are greenish white. The basal leaves are round and shiny.

SIDE-FLOWERED MITERWORT

WHERE FOUND:
Moist woods and meadows.

FLOWERING SEASON:
May to July.

Saxifrage Family
Mitella stauropetala

COMMENTS: (¼")
The toothed leaves are clustered at the base. At higher elevations the flower will arrive early, often when snow is still around.

WHITE SWEET CLOVER

WHERE FOUND:
Disturbed areas, roadsides.

FLOWERING SEASON:
June to August.

Pea Family
Melilotus alba

COMMENTS:
The plant exudes a sweet odor, especially when cut. The plant is grown as a cover crop and as forage. It imparts a pleasant odor to honey and is a favorite food of mule deer.

YELLOW	OTHER POSSIBLE COLORS
Avalanche Lily	white
Collomia	red
Columbine	blue
Coralroot	orange, purple
Fairybell	white
Fawn Lily	white
Fernleaf Lomatium	lavender
Foxglove	white, lavender
Groundsel	white
Honeysuckle	white, orange, red
Indian Paint Brush	white, orange, red
Lady's Slipper	white, pink
Lupine	blue
Mariposa	white, lavender
Parrot's Beak	white, pink, lavender
Wallflower	orange
Wood Sorrel	white, lavender
Violet	white, red, lavender, blue

YELLOW — NO PETALS

RABBITBRUSH

Composite Family
Chrysothamnus nauseosus

WHERE FOUND:
Dry, open areas.

FLOWERING SEASON:
July to October.

COMMENTS:
The generic name means goldenbush. While ray flowers are absent, there are many minute disk flowers. The alternate leaves have a disagreeable odor. Indians used the shrub for medicine, dyes and fuel. It furnishes browse for rabbits, sheep, deer and elk.

YELLOW — 2 PETALS (BRACTS)

LEAFY SPURGE

Spurge Family
Euphorbia esula

WHERE FOUND:
Roadsides, fields and disturbed areas.

FLOWERING SEASON:
June to August.

COMMENTS:
The minute true flowers are cupped in a bell-shaped pair of yellow-green bracts. The plant spreads by underground runners and is very hard to kill. All parts of the plant have a white, milky fluid which can produce blisters in humans and is poisonous to cattle. Leafy Spurge is listed as a noxious weed in several states.

YELLOW — 4 PETALS

BLACK MUSTARD

Mustard Family
Brassica Nigra

WHERE FOUND:
Roadsides and open fields.

FLOWERING SEASON:
May to August.

COMMENTS: (½")
The young leaves may be cooked and eaten as greens. The seeds of *B. nigra* contain an oil used to flavor our common table mustard. To release the flavor the seeds need a liquid, so the Romans added "must", or unfermented wine, to the chopped seeds to make a condiment. Germanic tribes called such a condiment mustard, meaning "hard must".

RABBITBRUSH

BLACK MUSTARD

LEAFY SPURGE

WESTERN WALLFLOWER

WINTER CRESS

BIRDFOOT TREFOIL

BITTERBRUSH

WESTERN WALLFLOWER

WHERE FOUND:
Dry rocky areas.

FLOWERING SEASON:
March to June.

Mustard Family
Erysimum cheiranthoides

COMMENTS: (½")
The Western Wallflowers are similar to domestic Wallflowers. They may be yellow or orange to orange-red. The zesty-tasting radish, horseradish, turnip and watercress are members of this family of flowers.

WINTER CRESS

WHERE FOUND:
Moist woods, fields, and waste places.

FLOWERING SEASON:
April to August.

Mustard Family
Barbarea orthoceras

COMMENTS: (⅜")
The leaves may be used as a salad plant, but are too bitter during flowering season.

BIRDFOOT TREFOIL

WHERE FOUND:
Roadsides and meadows.

FLOWERING SEASON:
June to August.

Pea Family
Lotus corniculatus

COMMENTS: (¼")
Birdfoot Trefoil was imported from Europe and grows across the United States. Most North American species grow only in the western states. There are three small leaflets at the tip of a short stem, plus two tiny "leaflets" at the stem base.

BITTERBRUSH

WHERE FOUND:
Dry soil up to 8000'.

FLOWERING SEASON:
May to July.

Rose Family
Purshia tridentata

COMMENTS: (½")
This flower grows on a shrub 2-10 feet tall, with a delightful odor and up to 25 stamen. *Tridentata* refers to the three-lobed leaf. Also known as Antelope Brush, the plant is a good browse for animals.

BUTTERCUP

WHERE FOUND:
Rocky high meadows and marshy areas.

FLOWERING SEASON:
February to August.

Buttercup Family
Ranunculus Sp.

COMMENTS: (½")
There are more than 300 varieties of the Buttercup, making it difficult to distinguish one from the other. The flower also may have more than five petals. The leaves are mildly poisonous when eaten raw. The seeds were once ground into meal for bread. The roots were boiled and eaten.

CINQUEFOIL

WHERE FOUND:
Moist meadows and woodlands.

FLOWERING SEASON:
May to August.

Rose Family
Potentilla Sp.

COMMENTS: (5/8")
Cinquefoil means five fingers and refers to the five-lobed leaves and not to the five petals of the flower. There are many species, so much alike that it can be difficult to differentiate between them. Some contain tannic acid and have been used as astringents.

COLLOMIA

WHERE FOUND:
Open woods, drier open hillsides.

FLOWERING SEASON:
May to July.

Phlox Family
Collomia grandiflora

COMMENTS: (1")
Petals are salmon to yellowish. There are some half-dozen species in the Northwest. The seeds have a mucus covering. When the seeds are dropped into water, the mucus diffuses and forms a smokelike cloud around the seeds.

GOLDEN COLUMBINE

WHERE FOUND:
Moist shaded areas.

FLOWERING SEASON:
June to August.

Buttercup Family
Aquilegia flavescens

COMMENTS: (2½")
Columbine comes from the Latin word for dove, and *aquilegia* is Latin for eagle. The names were inspired by the bird-like appearance of the flowers. The blue Columbine is Colorado's state flower.

BUTTERCUP

CINQUEFOIL

COLLOMIA

GOLDEN COLUMBINE

GROMWELL

LANCE-LEAVED STONECROP

MONKEY FLOWER

MUSK FLOWER

GROMWELL

Borage Family
Lithospermum ruderale

WHERE FOUND:
Dry fields and open woods.

FLOWERING SEASON:
May to June.

COMMENTS: (½")
The Gromwell is also called Stone Seed or Fringed Puccoon. Some species were used as a medicine. The roots were used for food by western Indians.

LANCE-LEAVED STONECROP

Sedum Family
Sedum lanceolatum

WHERE FOUND:
Dry rocky areas.

FLOWERING SEASON:
June to August.

COMMENTS: (⅛")
Stonecrops can survive in dry areas because their fleshy leaves store water. Furthermore, their leaf pores open at night, then close during the day, thereby conserving moisture. Both the stem leaves and the basal leaves are linear or lance-like.

MONKEY FLOWER

Figwort Family
Mimulus guttatus

WHERE FOUND:
Wet meadows, ditches, and along streams.

FLOWERING SEASON:
May to September.

COMMENTS: (1¼")
Also called Common Monkey Flower and Seep-Spring Monkey Flower, the plant has opposite, oval and slightly toothed leaves. *Guttatus* means speckled and refers to the tiny red dots on the lower petal. Indians and early settlers used the leaves for greens.

MUSK FLOWER

Figwort Family
Mimulus moschatus

WHERE FOUND:
Moist shaded areas and streamsides.

FLOWERING SEASON:
May to September.

COMMENTS: (¾")
A creeping plant with hairy leaves that feel slimy when wet. The Musk Flower is often confused with the Monkey Flowers, which are also in the *Mimulus* family.

RED TWINBERRY

Honeysuckle Family
Lonicera utahensis

WHERE FOUND:
Moist to drier soils of fields and woods.

FLOWERING SEASON:
May to July.

COMMENTS: (½")
Red Twinberry is a shrub with yellow flowers and bright red juicy berries which are edible but bitter. It is also called Utah Honeysuckle.

ST. JOHNSWORT

St. Johnswort Family
Hypericum perforatum

WHERE FOUND:
Moist meadows, roadsides and pastures.

FLOWERING SEASON:
June to September.

COMMENTS: (¾")
In England, this plant blooms about June 24, Midsummer's Day and the feast day of St. John the Baptist, hence the name. It is also called Klamath Weed. The plant is a very troublesome weed, but may be controlled by two European beetles that feed only on this species. Some American Indians used the plant to heal wounds.

SEDUM

Sedum Family
Sedum Sp.

WHERE FOUND:
Dry, open rocky areas.

FLOWERING SEASON:
June to August.

COMMENTS: (½")
There is a large variety of Sedum, all having similar characteristics. The word *Sedum* means "to sit" and refers to the tendency of most species to grow low to the ground. The plant requires little water to survive. Sedums include Jade Trees.

WOOD SORREL

Sorrel Family
Oxalis stricta

WHERE FOUND:
Open woods, fields, lawns, waste places.

FLOWERING SEASON:
All summer.

COMMENTS: (½")
The name Sorrel comes from the Old German word for sour and refers to the acrid juice of the plant. Sorrels were once used to treat stomach ailments, but they contain oxalic acid. Some species may be violet or white with pink stripes.

RED TWINBERRY

ST. JOHNSWORT

SEDUM

WOOD SORREL

YELLOW POND LILY

YELLOW VIOLET

BUCKWHEAT

GLACIER LILY

YELLOW POND LILY

Water Lily Family
Nuphar polysepalum

WHERE FOUND:
Shallow waters of streams, ponds and lakes.

FLOWERING SEASON:
June to August.

COMMENTS:
Also called Spatterdock. There is only one species in the West. Indians ate the roasted seeds, called "wokas", like popcorn.

YELLOW VIOLET

Violet Family
Viola glabella

WHERE FOUND:
Moist woods and meadows near water.

FLOWERING SEASON:
April to June.

COMMENTS: (1")
All species of Violet are edible. The young leaves and flower buds are used for salads or boiled as potherbs. Although the color "violet" was named after the flower, it is obvious that not all Violets are violet.

YELLOW 6 PETALS

BUCKWHEAT

Buckwheat Family
Eriogonum ovalifolium

WHERE FOUND:
Dry rocky areas.

FLOWERING SEASON:
May to July.

COMMENTS:
What appear to be petals are really sepals. The plant bears small resemblance to the cultivated grain. Birds and rodents eat the seeds. The name *Eriogonum* is derived from *erion*, meaning wool, and *gonum*, meaning knee.

GLACIER LILY

Lily Family
Erythronium grandiflorum

WHERE FOUND:
Mountain woods and meadows.

FLOWERING SEASON:
April to July.

COMMENTS: (2")
The Glacier Lily is often called Dogtooth Violet or Yellow Fawn Lily. It is closely related to the Avalanche Lily. Both the leaves and bulbs were eaten by the Indians. The tips (called anthers) of the stamen are sometimes red, sometimes yellow.

OREGON GRAPE

Barberry Family
Berberis repens

WHERE FOUND:
Open woodlands.

FLOWERING SEASON:
April to July.

COMMENTS: (½")
Bears like the sour berries of this shrub. Humans add sugar for both juice and jelly. The Indians used the stems and roots for a dye. One species is the state flower of Oregon.

YELLOW BELL

Lily Family
Fritillaria pudica

WHERE FOUND:
Open woods and meadows.

FLOWERING SEASON:
April to June.

COMMENTS: (½")
This flower is often called Yellow Fritillary or Goldcup. The bulbs are sought by bears, ground squirrels and gophers. They were eaten either raw or cooked by western Indians. The six "petals" are really three petals and three similar sepals.

YELLOW MANY PETALS

ARNICA

Composite Family
Arnica latifolia

WHERE FOUND:
Open, moist woods.

FLOWERING SEASON:
May to August.

COMMENTS: (2")
All parts of the plant have been used in drugs. Note that *A. latifolia* has a plurality of flowers branching from a single stem. The more common Arnica, *A. cordifolia*, has a single flower on each stem. All Arnicas have opposed heart-shaped leaves.

ARROWLEAF BALSAMROOT

Composite Family
Balsamorhiza sagittata

WHERE FOUND:
Open dry woods and grasslands.

FLOWERING SEASON:
April to July.

COMMENTS: (4")
Western Indians boiled, dried, and ground the roots for medicine. The young leaves can be boiled or used raw in salads. The seeds may be roasted or ground into flour.

OREGON GRAPE

ARNICA ➢

YELLOW BELL

ARROWLEAF BALSAMROOT ➢

BLACK-EYED SUSAN

BLANKET FLOWER

BOG MICROSERIS

DANDELION

BLACK-EYED SUSAN

Composite Family
Rudbeckia hirta

WHERE FOUND:
Open woods and meadows.

FLOWERING SEASON:
June to October.

COMMENTS: (3")
The Black-eyed Susan is one form of Coneflower, which is found nationwide. It is the state flower of Maryland. Parts of some species of *Rudbeckia* were used as a remedy for indigestion. The leaves of this species are alternate, hairy and smooth edged.

BLANKET FLOWER

Composite Family
Gaillardia aristata

WHERE FOUND:
Dry slopes and meadows.

FLOWERING SEASON:
June to August.

COMMENTS: (2")
The Blanket Flower has been domesticated as a garden flower. It is also called Brown-eyed Susan. The ray flowers are sometimes reddish at the base. The leaves, on the lowest part of the stem, are lance-shaped and may be six inches long.

BOG MICROSERIS

Composite Family
Microseris nutans

WHERE FOUND:
Marshy areas at higher elevations.

FLOWERING SEASON:
July to August.

COMMENTS:
This flower is related to our common blue Chicory. It opens during the morning hours.

DANDELION

Composite Family
Taraxacum officinale

WHERE FOUND:
Fields, meadows, woods and lawns.

FLOWERING SEASON:
April to October.

COMMENTS: (1")
This is one of the hardiest of wild flowers. The root has been used as a medicine for centuries. The tender leaves, which have sharp reverse lobes, may be used as a potherb. The flowers make a delicate wine. The name Dandelion derives from the French *dent de lion*, meaning the tooth of the lion, referring to the jagged, tooth-like edges of the leaves.

FALSE DANDELION

Composite Family
Agoseris glauca

WHERE FOUND:
Meadows and roadsides at most elevations.

FLOWERING SEASON:
May to August.

COMMENTS: (1¼")
There are about a dozen species, all having milky sap like true Dandelions. The leaves are basal, slender and toothed. *Glauca* means waxy, referring to the sap as it thickens on exposure to air.

FERNLEAF LOMATIUM

Parsley or Carrot Family
Lomatium dissectum

WHERE FOUND:
Dry, rocky areas.

FLOWERING SEASON:
April to June.

COMMENTS:
Each tiny flower in the umbels actually has five petals. The plant is also called Desert Parsley. The flower may be yellow or lavender. The roots of many species were eaten by Indians.

GOLDENROD

Composite Family
Solidago Sp.

WHERE FOUND:
Dry fields, woods and roadsides.

FLOWERING SEASON:
June to September.

COMMENTS:
There are about 25 species in the Northwest, very difficult to differentiate. Goldenrod is blamed for hay fever, but its pollen is too heavy to be windborne. The true culprits are Ragweed and other wind-pollenated plants. The Goldenrod is the state flower of both Kentucky and Nebraska.

GROUNDSEL

Composite Family
Senecio integerrimus

WHERE FOUND:
Medium-dry areas from prairies into the mountains.

FLOWERING SEASON:
May to August.

COMMENTS: (½")
The more than 1000 species of Groundsel typically have many flower heads topping the stem, with yellow disk flowers and rays. The leaves are oval to lance-shaped near the base of the stem and progressively smaller up the stem. While some species contain poisonous alkalis, the plant has been used medicinally.

FALSE DANDELION

FERNLEAF LOMATIUM

GOLDENROD

GROUNDSEL

HEARTLEAF ARNICA

HOP CLOVER

LEWIS'S LOMATIUM

MULE EARS

HEARTLEAF ARNICA

Composite Family
Arnica cordifolia

WHERE FOUND:
Open woodlands.

FLOWERING SEASON:
May to August

COMMENTS: (3")
Most Western species have an aromatic odor. All parts of the plant have been used in drugs. A tincture made from dried flower heads has been used as a treatment for sprains and bruises.

HOP CLOVER

Pea Family
Trifolium agrarium

WHERE FOUND:
Roadsides and disturbed areas.

FLOWERING SEASON:
June to August.

COMMENTS:
Hop Clover, also called Yellow Clover, is not easily recognized as a clover, but the leaves are divided into three parts. The flowers form tiny yellow "beehive" shaped heads, each containing thirty to forty seeds.

LEWIS'S LOMATIUM

Parsley or Carrot Family
Lomatium triternatum

WHERE FOUND:
Open meadows and dry, rocky forest openings.

FLOWERING SEASON:
April to July.

COMMENTS:
Each of the tiny flowers in the umbels actually has five petals. This Lomatium has tall grasslike basal leaves. It is also called Narrow-leaved Desert Parsley. Indians and early settlers made flour from the roots.

MULE EARS

Composite Family
Wyethia amplexicaulis

WHERE FOUND:
Open hillsides and meadows.

FLOWERING SEASON:
May to July.

COMMENTS: (2")
This plant is named for its long, glossy aromatic leaves, which may be over 12 inches long. Indians used the root as food. *Wyethia* is named for a Captain Wyeth who established the first trading post in the Northwest.

NARROWLEAF HAWKWEED

Composite Family
Hieracium pratense

WHERE FOUND:
Roadsides and open areas.

FLOWERING SEASON:
June to August.

COMMENTS: (1")
Like other Hawkweeds, the stems contain a milky juice. Most species of Hawkweed are eaten by livestock as well as game animals.

PRICKLY LETTUCE

Composite Family
Lactuca serriola

WHERE FOUND:
Roadsides and disturbed areas.

FLOWERING SEASON:
June to September.

COMMENTS: (½")
The plant grows to ten feet tall. The upper leaves are slender, while the lower leaves are broad, deeply lobed, with prickly edges. Prickly Lettuce is sometimes called Compass Plant; the margins of the leaves are arranged in a generally north-south direction, thereby avoiding the direct rays of the noon sun.

PRICKLY PEAR CACTUS

Cactus Family
Opuntia polyacantha

WHERE FOUND:
Dry, hot areas.

FLOWERING SEASON:
May to July.

COMMENTS: (½")
Cacti prevent loss of water in dry periods by dropping their spines (leaves). The fleshy plant stores water during rainy periods. The fruit of the flower may be used for jelly.

SOW THISTLE

Composite Family
Sonchus oleraceus

WHERE FOUND: Roadsides and waste areas.

FLOWERING SEASON: July to October.

COMMENTS: (1")
Oleraceus refers to potherbs, which may be used in salads or cooked. The leaves are spatula-shaped, have prickly edges, and clasp the stem of the plant.

NARROWLEAF HAWKWEED

PRICKLY LETTUCE

PRICKLY PEAR CACTUS

SOW THISTLE

SUNFLOWER

TANSY

WESTERN HAWKWEED

WESTERN SALSIFY
FLOWER ➢
SEED ➣

SUNFLOWER

Composite Family
Helianthus annuus

WHERE FOUND:
Roadsides, meadows and disturbed places.

FLOWERING SEASON:
June to September.

COMMENTS: (4")
This common variety, the state flower of Kansas, when cultivated may reach heights of 20 feet. Sunflower seeds are edible. Sunflower oil is valuable in cooking and in many food products. The seeds attract seed-eating birds.

TANSY

Composite Family
Tanacctum vulgare

WHERE FOUND:
Disturbed open areas.

FLOWERING SEASON:
June to September.

COMMENTS: (½")
The oils of the flower were believed to cause abortions. The crushed leaves were used in poultices for sprains and bruises. It has a bitter taste, so the plant is sometimes called Bitter Buttons. Farmers consider it a noxious weed.

WESTERN HAWKWEED

Composite Family
Hieracium albertinum

WHERE FOUND:
Fields and open woods.

FLOWERING SEASON:
June to August.

COMMENTS: (¾")
There are several species of Hawkweed, one having large basal leaves and almost bare stems, others having leaves running up the stem. The stems and other parts are covered with short hairs. Most species are eaten by livestock and game animals. It is also called Hairy Albert.

WESTERN SALSIFY

Composite Family
Tragopogon dubius

WHERE FOUND:
Open fields and slopes.

FLOWERING SEASON:
May to July.

COMMENTS: (3")
The flower and the seed head are beautiful. The flowers are open only in the morning. Early settlers introduced the plant as a food source because the roots are edible raw or cooked. The plants spread, and were soon used extensively by the Indians. The plant is also known as Goatsbeard or Oyster Plant, because the root is thought to taste like oysters.

BUTTER AND EGGS

Figwort/Snapdragon Family
Linaria vulgaris

WHERE FOUND:
Open fields and hillsides.

FLOWERING SEASON:
June to September.

COMMENTS:
The name Butter and Eggs refers to the flower being yellow with an orange throat. The flower is two-lipped with a long trailing spur, and is also called Common Toadflax.

DALMATIAN TOADFLAX

Figwort/Snapdragon Family
Linaria dalmatica

WHERE FOUND:
Open fields and disturbed areas.

FLOWERING SEASON:
May to September.

COMMENTS:
This flower is similar to Butter and Eggs but does not have an orange throat. The flower's nectar is contained in the long spur which indicates that the pollinators are humming birds or long-tongued insects.

FALSE LUPINE

Pea Family
Thermopsis montana

WHERE FOUND:
Open woodlands and meadows.

FLOWERING SEASON:
April to July.

COMMENTS:
This flower is also called Yellow Pea or Golden Pea. It is very similar to a true Lupine except that it has separate stamen and three leaflets, whereas the true Lupine has fused stamen and five or more leaflets. The plant is poisonous to cattle and humans.

MOTH MULLEIN

Figwort Family
Verbascum blattaria

WHERE FOUND:
Fields, roadsides and disturbed places.

FLOWERING SEASON:
July to October.

COMMENTS: (1")
This flower was introduced from Europe. In contrast to the dense spike of flowers on *V. thapsus*, the Moth Mullein flowers are sparsely spaced along the stem. The stamen are violet and fuzzy. The lower leaves are lance-shaped and notched while the leaves higher on the stem are smooth edged.

BUTTER AND EGGS

DALMATIAN TOADFLAX

FALSE LUPINE

MOTH MULLEIN

MULLEIN

SKUNK CABBAGE

YELLOW SWEET CLOVER

MULLEIN

Figwort Family
Verbascum thapsus

WHERE FOUND:
Dry sandy waste areas, roadsides and meadows.

FLOWERING SEASON:
June to September.

COMMENTS: (¾")
The Mullein has been used for medicinal purposes for hundreds of years. Its tea has a slightly sedative effect. The flower oil was used for earache and coughs. The leaves, which are elliptical and hairy, have been used to make skin lotions. They were also dried and smoked by some Indians. The Romans covered the stalks with suet and burned them as torches. The individual flowers have five petals.

SKUNK CABBAGE

Arum Family
Lysichitum americanum

WHERE FOUND:
Marshes, wet woods, along streams.

FLOWERING SEASON:
April to June.

COMMENTS:
Also called American Skunk Cabbage. The envelope-like cover surrounding the spike of flowers is called a spathe. The spike carries hundreds of minute flowers. The leaves may grow to five feet long. The plant has an unpleasant odor, but is eaten by black bears.

YELLOW SWEET CLOVER

Pea Family
Melilotus officinalis

WHERE FOUND:
Disturbed areas and roadsides.

FLOWERING SEASON:
June to August.

COMMENTS:
Also called Honey Clover, the plant on hot days exudes a sweet odor. The trifoliate leaves have toothed edges. Another species, *M. indica*, has leaves with teeth only above the middle. The plant is grown as a cover crop, as bee plants, and as forage.

ORANGE	OTHER POSSIBLE COLORS
Coralroot	yellow, purple
Honeysuckle	white, yellow, red
Indian Paint Brush	white, yellow, red
Wallflower	yellow

CALIFORNIA POPPY

Poppy Family
Eschscholzia californica

WHERE FOUND:
Open grasslands and hillsides.

FLOWERING SEASON:
March to September.

COMMENTS: (1½")
This lovely flower closes at night and on cloudy days. It has a spicy fragrance and is the state flower of California. It is an introduced flower in areas other than the Colorado River Gorge and Southern California.

HONEYSUCKLE

Honeysuckle Family
Lonicera ciliosa

WHERE FOUND:
Open woods and hillsides.

FLOWERING SEASON:
May to August.

COMMENTS:
Honeysuckle is a climbing vine, and the blossoms may be orange, white, yellow or red. The berries following the blossoms provide food for birds and bears. While they are not poisonous to humans, they are not very tasty. The sweet nectar, however, is said to be delightful.

ORANGE 6 PETALS

TIGER LILY

Lily Family
Lilium columbianum

WHERE FOUND:
Prairies and open woods.

FLOWERING SEASON:
May to August.

COMMENTS: (4")
One of the loveliest of western flowers, it is often transplanted to gardens. Note the typical purple spots on the curled-back petals.

CALIFORNIA POPPY

⮝ HONEYSUCKLE BERRY
HONEYSUCKLE ⮟

TIGER LILY

MERTEN'S CORALROOT

SPOTTED CORALROOT

STRIPED CORALROOT

MERTEN'S CORALROOT

Orchid Family
Corallorhiza mertensiana

WHERE FOUND:
Shaded coniferous forests.

FLOWERING SEASON:
May to July.

COMMENTS:
The Coralroot does not make its own food, but lives off dead plant material in the soil. The name refers to the branching root which is really a stem for the flower stalk. Each flower of the raceme has six petals. The lip petal has red lines.

SPOTTED CORALROOT

Orchid Family
Corallorhiza maculata

WHERE FOUND:
Moist shady woods.

FLOWERING SEASON:
April to September.

COMMENTS: (½")
The Coralroot does not make its own food, but lives off dead plant material in the soil. The name refers to the branching root which is really a stem for the flower stalk. The color ranges from orange to purplish. Note the spotted white lip.

STRIPED CORALROOT

Orchid Family
Corallorhiza striata

WHERE FOUND:
Moist shady woods.

FLOWERING SEASON:
May to August.

COMMENTS: (¾")
The Coralroot does not make its own food, but lives off dead plant material in the soil. The name refers to the branching root which is really a stem for the flower stalk. The color ranges from yellow to orange to purple. Note the pinkish stripes on the petals.

RED-PINK	OTHER POSSIBLE COLORS
Avalanche Lily	white, yellow
Blue-eyed Grass	white, lavender, blue
Collomia	yellow
Fleabane	white, lavender
Fireweed	lavender
Honeysuckle	white, yellow, orange
Indian Paint Brush	white, yellow, orange
Kinnikinnick	white
Lady's Slipper	white, yellow
Larkspur	white, purple, blue
Miner's Lettuce	white
Parrot's Beak	white, lavender
Penstemon	white, lavender, blue
Pinedrops	white
Phlox	white, lavender, blue
Siberian Lettuce	white
Skullcap	white, blue
Spearmint	lavender
Spring Beauty	white
Trillium	white, purple
Violet	white, yellow, lavender, blue
Wild Sweet Pea	white, lavender
Wild Clover	white

RED-PINK — NO PETALS

MEADOW RUE

WHERE FOUND:
Moist meadows and shaded woods.

FLOWERING SEASON:
May to August.

Buttercup Family
Thalictrum occidentale

COMMENTS: (3/8")
The flowers are tiny but the plant may be five feet tall. Five green sepals may appear to be petals. Some species have male and female flowers on the same plant, but this species always has male and female flowers on separate plants. The female flower is greenish-white.

RED-PINK — 4 PETALS

FOOL'S HUCKLEBERRY

WHERE FOUND:
Moist woods, medium to subalpine altitudes.

FLOWERING SEASON:
May to August.

Heath Family
Menziesia ferruginea

COMMENTS: (¼")
The flower has four lobed petals and urn-shaped flowers in terminal clusters. The leaves of this shrub are alternate, elliptical and finely toothed. The flower may be confused with the huckleberry, except that this plant does not produce berries.

RED-PINK — 5 PETALS

ALPINE LAUREL

WHERE FOUND:
Wet areas and sphagnum bogs at higher elevations.

FLOWERING SEASON:
June to September.

Heath Family
Kalmia microphylla

COMMENTS: (½")
The species is named after a Swedish botanist. It is a low-lying shrub with opposite leathery leaves, dark green on the upper side and grayish on the lower side. The plant may be poisonous.

MEADOW RUE (MALE)

MEADOW RUE (FEMALE)

FOOL'S HUCKLEBERRY

ALPINE LAUREL

CAROLINA GERANIUM

COLLOMIA

DEPTFORD PINK

DWARF MONKEY FLOWER

CAROLINA GERANIUM

Geranium Family
Geranium carolinianum

WHERE FOUND:
Woods and meadows.

FLOWERING SEASON:
May to August.

COMMENTS:
Note the five-lobed notched leaves, typical of the Geranium family. The seed pods build up pressure as they dry and burst violently to spray seeds up to twenty feet.

COLLOMIA

Phlox Family
Collomia linearis

WHERE FOUND:
Open moist areas.

FLOWERING SEASON:
May to August.

COMMENTS: (¼" - ½")
The flowers are in a dense terminal head but sometimes appear in the leaf axils in a smaller size. All species are native to western North America. The genus name comes from the word *kolla*, meaning glue.

DEPTFORD PINK

Pink Family
Dianthus armeria

WHERE FOUND:
Roadsides and meadows.

FLOWERING SEASON:
May to August.

COMMENTS: (1")
The flower, also called Grass Pink, was named for the frilled or "pinked" appearance of the petals. The color pink was later named after the flower. This species was named for the old English town of Deptford, where the flowers once flourished.

DWARF MONKEY FLOWER

Figwort Family
Mimulus nanus

WHERE FOUND:
Dry areas.

FLOWERING SEASON:
May to August.

COMMENTS: (¾")
The flower grows in low-lying mats. The throat has dark lines and two yellow-haired ridges.

INDIAN PAINT BRUSH

WHERE FOUND:
Moist soils at most elevations.

FLOWERING SEASON:
May to September.

Figwort Family
Castilleja miniata

COMMENTS: (1¼")
There are more than 45 species in the West. The brightly colored bracts are mistaken for the hidden flower petals. Colors may be white, yellow, orange or red, but most of us only recognize the red variety. Paint Brush is the state flower of Wyoming.

MILKWEED

WHERE FOUND:
Open meadows and fields.

FLOWERING SEASON:
June to August.

Milkweed Family
Asclepias speciosa

COMMENTS:
The name *Asclepias* comes from Asklepios, the Greek god of medicine. Milkweed has long been used in medicines. The leaves are poisonous to most animals, but are not so to Monarch caterpillars. By eating the leaves, the caterpillars and subsequent butterflies become toxic to predators.

LONG LEAVED PHLOX

WHERE FOUND:
Dry rocky areas.

FLOWERING SEASON:
May to July.

Phlox Family
Phlox longifolia

COMMENTS: (¾")
There are many species of Phlox. This lovely upright species has lance-shaped or linear leaves. The corolla tube is twice the length of the sepals and the style is shorter than the corolla tube. The word *Phlox* means fire in Greek.

MOUNTAIN PHLOX

WHERE FOUND:
Dry, open rocky foothills and open woods.

FLOWERING SEASON:
May to November.

Phlox Family
Phlox diffusa

COMMENTS: (½")
Also called Spreading Phlox. It may be white or lavender. The garden variety of Phlox is often called Sweet William.

INDIAN PAINT BRUSH

MILKWEED

LONG LEAVED PHLOX

MOUNTAIN PHLOX

PHLOX

PRAIRIE SMOKE

RED FLOWERING CURRANT

SCARLET GILIA

PHLOX

WHERE FOUND:
Dry, gravelly areas.

FLOWERING SEASON:
May to August.

Phlox Family
Phlox Sp.

COMMENTS: (¾")
There are numerous species, very difficult to distinguish. Petals may be white, pink, blue or lavender. The flowers have a delicate fragrance, but the prickly opposed leaves are ignored by most animals. Phlox means fire in Greek.

PRAIRIE SMOKE

WHERE FOUND:
Open fields and hillsides.

FLOWERING SEASON:
April to August.

Rose Family
Geum triflorum

COMMENTS: (¾")
The long feathery tails are part of the fruit. The seeds have long filaments which are carried far by the wind. The bulbs are edible. The leaves are dainty and narrowly cleft. The flower is also called Long-plumed Avens. It is interesting that when the flower first blooms, it hangs downward like a bell. After it has been fertilized, it turns upward.

RED FLOWERING CURRANT

WHERE FOUND:
Open to wooded areas.

FLOWERING SEASON:
May to July.

Gooseberry Family
Ribes sanguineum

COMMENTS:
The Red Flowering Currant is a woody shrub. The petals of the flower are smaller and less showy than the sepals. The black berries are unpalatable.

SCARLET GILIA

WHERE FOUND:
Rocky sandy slopes.

FLOWERING SEASON:
May to September.

Phlox Family
Gilia aggregata

COMMENTS:
This flower is also called Skyrocket for obvious reasons. Because the crushed leaves have such a strong odor, it is also sometimes referred to as Skunk Flower.

SHOWY PHLOX

Phlox Family
Phlox speciosa

WHERE FOUND:
Open fields and forests.

FLOWERING SEASON:
April to June.

COMMENTS: (¾")
The loose clusters of pink flowers have deeply lobed petals. The word Phlox means fire in Greek.

SKULLCAP

Mint Family
Scutellaria galericulata

WHERE FOUND:
Moist woods and wet meadows.

FLOWERING SEASON:
May to June.

COMMENTS:
There are several species of Skullcap, which may be pink, white or blue. The name derives from the tiny crest on the calyx (behind the petals). It was once believed that the plant could be used to cure nervous disorders and convulsions.

SNOWBERRY

Honeysuckle Family
Symphoricarpus albus

WHERE FOUND:
Open hillsides, riverbanks, moist areas.

FLOWERING SEASON:
April to June.

COMMENTS:
There are four species of Snowberry in the West. All are similar in appearance with their pinkish tubular flowers and distinctive white berries, which survive through the winter. Though considered to be poisonous to humans, the berries are a valuable food source for birds. The deer browse on the foliage. Some Indian tribes used the stems and roots as emergency food.

SPREADING DOGBANE

Dogbane Family
Apocynum androsaemifolium

WHERE FOUND:
Roadsides and dry shaded foothills.

FLOWERING SEASON:
May to September.

COMMENTS: (¼")
The flowers are fragrant bells but the leaves have a strong taste. The flower's name arose from an early belief that it was poisonous to dogs. Indians made nets of cloth from fibers of the stems, as well as a cough medicine and an earache remedy from the roots.

SHOWY PHLOX

SKULLCAP

< SPREADING DOGBANE

SNOWBERRY
(FLOWER AND BERRIES)

STICKY GERANIUM

STORK'S-BILL

TWIN FLOWER

WILD ROSE

STICKY GERANIUM

Geranium Family
Geranium viscosissimum

WHERE FOUND:
Moist soil of fields and woods.

FLOWERING SEASON:
May to August.

COMMENTS: (1")
The foliage is hairy and sticky. The leaves have five to seven pointed lobes. It is a valuable forage plant and a major food source for elk, deer and bears.

STORK'S-BILL

Geranium Family
Erodium cicutarium

WHERE FOUND:
Pastures and meadows.

FLOWERING SEASON:
April to August.

COMMENTS: (½")
This delicate flower is also called Cranesbill or Red-Stemmed Filaree. The seed pods resemble stork's bills, hence the name. The leaves are deeply notched and toothed. It is a valuable forage plant and the young plants can be eaten as greens. Birds relish the seeds.

TWIN FLOWER

Honeysuckle Family
Linnaea borealis

WHERE FOUND:
Along streams and in moist shaded woods.

FLOWERING SEASON:
June to September.

COMMENTS:
The twin pink bells are delightfully fragrant. The plant makes a beautiful ground cover. Carolus Linnaeus of Sweden helped develop the system of combining a generic and a specific name to form the species name of plants and animals. It is said that the Twin Flower bears his name because it was his favorite flower.

WILD ROSE

Rose Family
Rosa nutkana

WHERE FOUND:
Open woods.

FLOWERING SEASON:
May to July.

COMMENTS: (2")
The fruit of the flower, called rose hips, is used to make tea, and is a valuable winter forage crop. This variety has five leaflets, whereas *R. woodsii* has seven to nine leaflets and the petals are a deeper pink.

RED-PINK — 5 PETALS

WILD SWEET PEA

WHERE FOUND:
Meadows and open woods.

FLOWERING SEASON:
April to July.

Pea Family
Lathyrus Sp.

COMMENTS:
The various species of the Wild Sweet Pea closely resemble the garden variety. The flowers shade from lavender to deep purple, pink to deep red, and off-white. Some species are edible; others may be toxic. The divided leaves have a tendril at the end for climbing.

RED-PINK — 6 PETALS

HOOKER'S ONION

WHERE FOUND:
Dry sunny areas.

FLOWERING SEASON:
June to July.

Lily Family
Allium acuminatum

COMMENTS: (½")
Note the three small inner petals and the three larger outer petal-like sepals. Both petals and sepals have turned-back tips. The short basal leaves are grasslike and barely noticeable.

WILD ONION

WHERE FOUND:
Moist meadows and rocky slopes.

FLOWERING SEASON:
May to July.

Lily Family
Allium Sp.

COMMENTS:
There are probably more than forty species of onion in the Northwest. All have the familiar odor and taste of onions. Ground squirrels feed on the plant's bulbs.

RED-PINK — MANY PETALS

KNAPWEED

WHERE FOUND:
Fields and roadsides.

FLOWERING SEASON:
June to September.

Composite Family
Centaurea maculosa

COMMENTS: (¾")
Spotted Knapweed, or Spotted Star Thistle, is known as a noxious weed. The leaves are alternate and deeply cleft. A garden variety, *Centaurea cyanus*, Cornflower or Bachelor's Button, is Germany's national flower.

WILD SWEET PEA

HOOKER'S ONION

WILD ONION

KNAPWEED

PUSSY TOES

WILD CLOVER

ELEPHANT HEAD

MOUNTAIN GLOBEMALLOW

PUSSY TOES

Composite Family
Antennaria anaphaloides

WHERE FOUND:
Dry to moist open areas.

FLOWERING SEASON:
April to June.

COMMENTS: (1/8")
Some species produce seeds without fertilization, and some have separate male and female parts. Gum prepared from the stalks was chewed by western Indians.

WILD CLOVER

Pea Family
Trifolium pratense

WHERE FOUND:
Moist meadows and hillsides.

FLOWERING SEASON:
May to July.

COMMENTS: (½")
The flower is also called Red Clover and is probably the most common of the clover family. A composite type of flower appearing to have many petals, each tiny flower in the head has five petals. All species of clover may be eaten raw, but are hard to digest unless cooked. Wild Clover is a valuable forage crop for grouse, deer, elk and bear.

RED-PINK — RACEME

ELEPHANT HEAD

Figwort/Snapdragon Family
Pedicularis groenlandica

WHERE FOUND:
Wet soils of meadows and bogs at higher elevations.

FLOWERING SEASON:
June to August.

COMMENTS: (5/8")
The name *Pedicularis* comes from the Latin word for louse. It was once believed that cattle eating the plant became infested with lice. *Groenlandica* means "from Greenland", but the plant is not believed to grow there.

MOUNTAIN GLOBEMALLOW

Mallow Family
Iliamna rivularis

WHERE FOUND:
Along streams and moist open areas.

FLOWERING SEASON:
June to August.

COMMENTS: (1½")
Each flower in the loose raceme has five petals. Color ranges from pink to deep red. Several species grow in the Northwest. It is also called Mountain Hollyhock.

PINK PYROLA

Wintergreen Family
Pyrola

WHERE FOUND:
Moist shaded areas.

FLOWERING SEASON:
June to August.

COMMENTS: (3/8")
Also called Bog Wintergreen. The basal leaves are evergreen and leathery. Because of the resemblance to the leaves of the pear tree, *pirus,* this plant was called *pyrola*, meaning "little pear tree". Each flower has five petals.

RED BESSEYA

Figwort/Snapdragon Family
Besseya rubra

WHERE FOUND:
Open rocky areas.

FLOWERING SEASON:
May to June.

COMMENTS:
The tiny flowers have no true corollas and grow in a dense fuzzy spike along the stem. The flower is named after American botanist Charles Bessey.

STEEPLEBUSH

Rose Family
Spiraea douglasii

WHERE FOUND:
Streamsides and moist meadows.

FLOWERING SEASON: July to September.

COMMENTS:
Each of the many minute flowers actually has five petals. Note the steeple-like shape of the flower clusters distinguishing Steeplebush from Pink Spirea, wherein the flowers are in elongated clusters close to the stem. Steeplebush is also known as Hardhack.

PINK PYROLA

RED BESSYA

STEEPLEBUSH

LAVENDER-PURPLE	OTHER POSSIBLE COLORS
Aster	white, blue
Blue-eyed Grass	white, pink, blue
Buckbrush	white, blue
Coralroot	yellow, orange
Fernleaf Lomatium	yellow
Field Mint	white
Fireweed	pink
Fleabane	white, pink
Foxglove	white, yellow
Grass Widow	blue
Larkspur	white, pink, blue
Mariposa	white, yellow
Parrot's Beak	white, yellow, pink
Penstemon	white, red, blue
Phlox	white, pink, blue
Spearmint	pink
Trillium	white, red
Violet	white, yellow, red, blue
Wild Sweet Pea	white, pink, red
Wood Sorrel	white, yellow

PURPLE TRILLIUM

WHERE FOUND:
Moist shaded areas.

FLOWERING SEASON:
April to June.

Lily Family
Trillium petiolatum

COMMENTS:
The flowers grow at the base of the large leaves and are fairly small. The large round leaves have petioles nearly as long as the leaves. The flowers therefore are almost hidden, so we should first look for the tell-tale leaves which may be four to five inches wide. The flower is also called the Roundleaf Trillium.

SAGEBRUSH MARIPOSA

WHERE FOUND:
Dry open areas.

FLOWERING SEASON:
June and July.

Lily Family
Calochortus macrocarpus

COMMENTS: (2")
This flower is also called Large Flowered Mariposa. Note the pale green stripe down the outside of each petal, and the triangular gland in an area of yellow hairs on the inside base of each petal between two maroon arced bands. The name *calochortus* comes from the Greek *kalos*, beautiful, plus *chortos*, grass, referring to the leaves. Mariposa is the Spanish word for butterfly, and the petals very often resemble the colorful wings of some butterflies.

WILD GINGER

WHERE FOUND:
Shady moist woods.

FLOWERING SEASON:
May to July.

Birthwort Family
Asarum caudatum

COMMENTS:
The strange-looking flowers hide beneath the long-stemmed heart-shaped leaves, and therefore may be hard to spot. The plant smells like ginger and the root stems, if boiled with sugar water, can be used as a substitute. The plant was used among American Indians as a medicinal herb. Modern research indicates that the roots contain an antibiotic substance.

PURPLE TRILLIUM

SAGEBRUSH MARIPOSA

WILD GINGER

CLARKIA

FIREWEED

CORN COCKLE

FIELD MINT

CLARKIA

Evening Primrose Family
Clarkia pulchella

WHERE FOUND:
Dry grasslands and foothills.

FLOWERING SEASON:
May to July.

COMMENTS: (1½")
Pulchella means beautiful. Clarkia was named after William Clark of the Lewis and Clark expedition. Note the three sharply defined lobes of each petal. The species shown is also called Deerhorn, distinguished by the middle lobe of each petal being twice as wide as each side lobe.

FIREWEED

Evening Primrose Family
Epilobium angustifolium

WHERE FOUND:
Prairies, open woods and burned areas.

FLOWERING SEASON:
June to September.

COMMENTS: (1")
This is one of the first plants to grow after a forest fire, hence its name. The petals range from pink to lavender to purple. Bees love the nectar. Young shoots may be eaten boiled or in salads, or dried for soup or tea.

LAVENDER-PURPLE 5 PETALS

CORN COCKLE

Pink Family
Agrostemma githago

WHERE FOUND:
Meadows and grain fields.

FLOWERING SEASON:
May to July.

COMMENTS: (1¼")
The Corn Cockle is a noxious weed. Its poisonous seeds can contaminate wheat. In Europe, the word "corn" denoted hard-seeded cereal plants such as wheat, oats and rye. Our "corn" should properly be called "maize".

FIELD MINT

Mint Family
Mentha arvensis

WHERE FOUND:
Wet fields, woods and stream banks.

FLOWERING SEASON:
July to September.

COMMENTS:
The flowers may be white to pale lavender, and grow in clusters at leaf bases. All mints may be used for making jelly or juleps. In mythology, Mentha was a Naiad who was trampled by the jealous Proserpine and changed into a plant.

NIGHTSHADE

Nightshade Family
Solanum dulcamara

WHERE FOUND:
Open woods and along streams.

FLOWERING SEASON:
April to September.

COMMENTS:
The species shown is distinguished by the opposed pointed lobes at the base of each leaf. It is known as Bittersweet Nightshade and may be slighly narcotic. Some species are believed to be poisonous, especially *Belladonna atropic*, a European plant.

PEPPERMINT

Mint Family
Mentha piperita

WHERE FOUND:
Moist disturbed areas, wet woods, and stream banks.

FLOWERING SEASON:
June to September.

COMMENTS:
Flowers are in dense clusters. The leaves are slightly rounded. Note their fragrance and hot taste. Peppermint is used for medicine, tea and flavoring, and in jelly or juleps. In mythology, Mentha was a Naiad who was trampled by the jealous Proserpine and transformed into a plant.

SELFHEAL

Mint Family
Prunella lanceolata

WHERE FOUND:
Fields, woods, and waste places.

FLOWERING SEASON:
May to September.

COMMENTS:
Also called Heal-All. The plant was once used in England as a poultice for wounds. It was also combined with catnip and used as a physic. This is the native American variety of Selfheal. The European variety is *P. vulgaris*, which has leaves that are more elliptical.

SHOOTING STAR

Primrose Family
Dodecatheon pulchellum

WHERE FOUND:
Moist open meadows.

FLOWERING SEASON:
April to May.

COMMENTS:
The genus name, *dodecatheon*, translates to "twelve gods". The roots and leaves of some species are edible. In one species, the nose tip is separated from the petals by a yellow band.

NIGHTSHADE

PEPPERMINT

SELFHEAL

SHOOTING STAR

VETCH

SPEARMINT

VIOLET

WHORLED PENSTEMON

SPEARMINT

Mint Family
Mentha spicata

WHERE FOUND:
Moist fields, meadows, woodlands and streamsides.

FLOWERING SEASON:
June to October.

COMMENTS:
The flowers grow in slender spikes and may be pink to pale violet. Note the lance-shaped toothed leaves. The oil of the leaves is said to repel insects. All mints may be used for making jelly or juleps. In mythology, Mentha was a Naiad who was trampled by the jealous Proserpine and transformed into a plant.

VETCH

Pea Family
Vicia americana

WHERE FOUND:
Grassy meadows, open woods, and roadsides.

FLOWERING SEASON:
April to August.

COMMENTS:
Like sweet peas, vetch climbs fences or stems of other plants by means of tendrils. The seeds are edible. There are over one hundred species, some used as a cover crop or as feed for cattle and sheep.

VIOLET

Violet Family
Viola Sp.

WHERE FOUND:
Meadows, hillsides, open woods.

FLOWERING SEASON:
April to July.

COMMENTS: (5/8")
Of about one hundred species in the United States, some twenty-five are in the West. Colors may be white, yellow, blue, red, violet, purple, or mixed. All are edible. The violet is the state flower of Illinois, Rhode Island, Wisconsin and New Jersey.

WHORLED PENSTEMON

Pentstemon Family
Penstemon fruticosis

WHERE FOUND:
Dry, rocky slopes.

FLOWERING SEASON:
June to July.

COMMENTS:
Of the five petals, two are fused into an upper lobe and three are fused into a lower lobe. All species have five stamen, of which one is sterile. This flower is called Beardtongue because one of the stamen is bearded.

FAIRY SLIPPER

Orchid Family
Calypso bulbosa

WHERE FOUND:
Moist coniferous woods, usually near decayed logs.

FLOWERING SEASON:
May to July.

COMMENTS:
This species is also called the Calypso Orchid. Calypso was the sea nymph who detained Odysseus for seven years during his return from the Trojan War. As in all Orchids, the "six petals" are really three petals and three sepals. Though there are some thousands of species throughout the world, they do not germinate readily, so each species is really quite rare.

PURPLE FRITILLARY

Lily Family
Fritillaria lanceolata

WHERE FOUND:
Open wooded areas.

FLOWERING SEASON:
March to June.

COMMENTS: (¾")
Also called Chocolate Lily, Checker Lily or Mission Bell. Despite the bright yellow stamen and the yellowish mottling on the insides of the petals, the flower is often overlooked because it hangs downward. All that is seen is the brownish-purple back of the petals.

LAVENDER-PURPLE MANY PETALS

ASTER

Composite Family
Aster Sp.

WHERE FOUND:
Meadows and open woods.

FLOWERING SEASON:
July to September.

COMMENTS:
There are over 2000 species in North America, varying in color from white to blue to deep purple. Asters are often confused with Daisies, but Asters bloom later, are taller and have several layers of overlapping bracts. The Daisy ray flowers are usually narrower and more numerous. Eastern American Indians used parts of certain Asters for food and medicine. *Aster* is the Greek word for star. The same root word brings us astronaut, astronomy, astrology and asterisk.

FAIRY SLIPPER

⮝ PURPLE FRITILLARY
INSIDE VIEW ⮟

ASTER

FLEABANE

THISTLE

FOXGLOVE

TEASEL (BLOOMING AND AFTER BLOOMING)

FLEABANE

Composite Family
Erigeron speciosus

WHERE FOUND:
Open areas.

FLOWERING SEASON:
May to August.

COMMENTS: (¾")
Also called Showy Daisy. There are at least thirty species of Fleabane in the West. The rays may be white, pink or lavender. They were once considered to be repellant to fleas.

THISTLE

Composite Family
Cirsium vulgare

WHERE FOUND:
Meadows, roadsides, and disturbed areas.

FLOWERING SEASON
May to September.

COMMENTS: (1¼")
This species is called the Bull Thistle. *Vulgare* means common, and this thistle certainly is. Thistle roots can be eaten raw or cooked. Water from boiled roots was once used for women's ailments. Thistledown makes a very good tinder.

FOXGLOVE

Figwort Family
Digitalis purpurea

WHERE FOUND:
Moist fields and streambanks.

FLOWERING SEASON:
June to September.

COMMENTS:
The leaves contain the powerful poison, digitalis, which can be fatal to children, but is useful in treating certain heart diseases. The petals are usually lavender, but may be white or yellow. The German name for Foxglove is *fingerhut*, meaning "finger hat" (thimble). When the flower was first classified, this reference to the finger suggested the Latin name *digitalis*, pertaining to the finger.

TEASEL

Composite Family
Dipsacus sylvestris

WHERE FOUND:
Fields and waste areas.

FLOWERING SEASON:
June to October.

COMMENTS:
Teasels were cultivated both in Europe and America for their spiny flowerheads. The heads were used on woolen cloth to tease, or raise, the nap of the cloth.The flower petals vary from pale lavender to white.

BLUE	OTHER POSSIBLE COLORS
Aster	white, lavender
Blue-eyed Grass	white, pink, lavender
Buckbrush	white, lavender
Columbine	yellow
Grass Widow	lavender, purple
Larkspur	white, pink, purple
Lupine	yellow
Penstemon	white, red, lavender, purple
Phlox	white, pink, lavender
Skullcap	white, pink
Violet	white, yellow, red, lavender
Wild Hyacinth	white

BLUE — 4 PETALS

CLEMATIS

Buttercup Family
Clematis columbiana

WHERE FOUND:
Moist woods.

FLOWERING SEASON:
April to July.

COMMENTS: (2½")
This beautiful, twining, climbing plant has no true petals, but the four sepals are petal-like. They are a lavender-blue color. The feathery styles that carry the seeds are easily ignited and make good tinder.

BLUE — 5 PETALS

BLUEBELL

Borage Family
Mertensia campanulata

WHERE FOUND:
Moist areas.

FLOWERING SEASON:
May to July.

COMMENTS:
The Bluebells are often confused with Lungworts, but the base of the Lungwort corolla tube tends to be pinkish. The species shown is often called the Tall Bluebell.

COMMON FLAX

Flax Family
Linum usitatissimum

WHERE FOUND:
Dry hills, open fields, and high ridges.

FLOWERING SEASON:
May to September.

COMMENTS: (1")
The leaves are linear and alternate along the stem. Indians ate the seeds roasted and ground. They used the stems for rope and fishing lines. The seed is used for linseed oil, while linen is made from flax fibers.

DWARF WATERLEAF

Waterleaf Family
Hydrophyllum capitatum

WHERE FOUND:
Moist shaded to open forests.

FLOWERING SEASON:
April to June.

COMMENTS:
Rainwater is caught and held in the cavity of the leaf, hence the name. The young shoots are delicious in salads. The roots are edible if cooked.

BLUEBELL

⮝ CLEMATIS
IN SEED ⮟

DWARF WATERLEAF

COMMON FLAX ➤

EUROPEAN BELLFLOWER

FORGET-ME-NOT

JACOB'S LADDER

LARKSPUR

EUROPEAN BELLFLOWER

Bluebell Family
Campanula rapunculoides

WHERE FOUND:
Rocky areas at higher elevations.

FLOWERING SEASON:
July to September.

COMMENTS:
This flower was brought from Europe to grace American gardens. It escaped and has become a pesky weed in some areas because it spreads by underground runners and can be difficult to eradicate.

FORGET-ME-NOT

Borage Family
Myosotis sylvatica

WHERE FOUND:
Moist shaded areas.

FLOWERING SEASON:
April to August.

COMMENTS: (¾")
There are several species, growing mostly in secluded rocky areas. The flowers are on diverging stems which uncoil as the flowers bloom. The Forget-me-not is the state flower of Alaska.

JACOB'S LADDER

Phlox Family
Polemonium pulcherrimum

WHERE FOUND:
Moist shaded areas.

FLOWERING SEASON:
June to August.

COMMENTS: (⅝")
The name is derived from the slender opposed leaves resembling the rungs of a ladder. The plant is also called Greek Valerian.

LARKSPUR

Buttercup Family
Delphinium nuttallianum

WHERE FOUND:
Well-drained open woods and prairies.

FLOWERING SEASON:
March to July.

COMMENTS:
This is the western species, but all of the species are recognizable by the backward projecting spur. Some species are poisonous to cattle. The Hopi Indians made a blue dye from the flowers, while early settlers used the extract to make ink. Larkspur may be blue, pink or white, and is often called by its Latin name, Delphinium.

NARROWLEAF SKULLCAP

Mint Family
Scutellaria angustifolia

WHERE FOUND:
Open rocky areas.

FLOWERING SEASON:
May to July.

COMMENTS:
This species of Skullcap is distinctive in that the tubular corolla is sharply bent near its base. The name derives from the tiny crest behind the petals.

PENSTEMON

Snapdragon Family
Penstemon procerus

WHERE FOUND:
Moist meadows and open slopes.

FLOWERING SEASON:
May to July.

COMMENTS:
Of the five petals, two are fused into an upper lobe, and three are fused into a lower lobe. All species have five stamen, of which one is sterile. The flower's name originally was Pentstemon, meaning five stamen. Petals may be white, red, blue, lavender or purple. Penstemon is also called Beardtongue, because one of the stamen is bearded.

PERIWINKLE

Dogbane Family
Vinca minor

WHERE FOUND:
Open fields.

FLOWERING SEASON:
March to June.

COMMENTS: (¾")
Periwinkle, which is also called Myrtle, was imported by early settlers, probably for medicinal purposes; however, it is not edible. The leaves and blossoms appear simultaneously in early spring.

ROUNDLEAF BLUEBELL

Bluebell Family
Campanula rotundifolia

WHERE FOUND:
Meadows and woods.

FLOWERING SEASON:
June to August.

COMMENTS: (¾")
This species is also called Harebell, or Bluebell of Scotland because the flower grows profusely there. The name *rotundifolia* refers to the round basal leaves of this species. However, the alternate stem leaves are linear. Eastern American Indians used the liquid from boiling the roots as an earache remedy.

NARROWLEAF SKULLCAP

PENSTEMON

PERIWINKLE

ROUNDLEAF BLUEBELL

TRUMPET ➢
LUNGWORT

WESTERN
MONKSHOOD

BLUE-EYED GRASS

TRUMPET LUNGWORT

Borage Family
Mertensia longiflora

WHERE FOUND:
Sunny open slopes.

FLOWERING SEASON:
April to June.

COMMENTS: (½")
Lungworts are often confused with Bluebells, and in some places are called Bluebells. The Lungwort was once thought to contain a remedy for lung diseases. There are several western species of *Mertensia.*

WESTERN MONKSHOOD

Buttercup Family
Aconitum columbianum

WHERE FOUND:
Moist woods and meadows.

FLOWERING SEASON:
June to August.

COMMENTS:
This flower is also called Aconite or Wolfbane. The name derives from the appearance of the hood, which covers two petals, and is similar to hoods worn by medieval monks. The seeds and roots of the plant are poisonous. The drug Aconite is used as a sedative.

BLUE 6 PETALS

BLUE-EYED GRASS

Iris Family
Sisyrinchium angustifolium

WHERE FOUND:
Moist open areas.

FLOWERING SEASON:
April to July.

COMMENTS:
The leaves of Blue-eyed Grass are so much like wild grasses that the flower is almost impossible to find unless it is in bloom. Colors range from white to blue to pink and lavender. Blue-eyed Grass is similar to the Grass Widow, except that the stamen of the latter are united for about half their length, while the stamen of Blue-eyed Grass are united for almost their entire length.

CAMAS

Lily Family
Camassia quamash

WHERE FOUND:
Open moist grassy areas.

FLOWERING SEASON: May to August

COMMENTS: (1½")
Basal leaves are grasslike. Camas bulbs were a very important food for the Nez Perce and Coeur d'Alene Indians. The bulbs were pit roasted or boiled.

GRASS WIDOW

Iris Family
Sisyrinchium inflatum

WHERE FOUND:
Moist open areas.

FLOWERING SEASON: April to July.

COMMENTS: (1")
Species can be hard to distinguish. There are other species closely resembling the one shown. Colors shade from blue to light purple to deep purple. The Grass Widow is similar to Blue-eyed Grass, *S. angustifolium*, except that the stamen of the former are united for about half their length while the stamen of Blue-eyed Grass are united for almost their entire length.

WILD HYACINTH

Lily Family
Brodiaea douglasii

WHERE FOUND:
Moist meadows and open woods.

FLOWERING SEASON:
May to July.

COMMENTS: (¾")
The bulbs are edible, either raw or cooked. They are widely considered to be the tastiest of the edible bulbs. Petals may be blue or white. The few basal leaves are grasslike.

CAMAS

GRASS WIDOW

WILD HYACINTH

CHICORY

LUPINE

CHICORY

Composite Family
Cichorium intybus

WHERE FOUND:
Open fields and roadsides.

FLOWERING SEASON:
June to October.

COMMENTS: (1")
Chicory spread from the Mediterranean area to many countries because the roots, if ground and roasted, could be used as a flavoring agent in, or used in place of, coffee. Though a composite, the blossom has no central disk. All of the elements are ray flowers. Chicory has also been called Blue Sailor.

BLUE RACEME

LUPINE

Pea Family
Lupinus Sp.

WHERE FOUND:
Open areas at all elevations.

FLOWERING SEASON:
May to July.

COMMENTS:
The leaves are distinctive, forming a many-fingered bowl. There are many species, including a yellow variety. The seeds are a valuable food for game birds. Lupine grows well in poor soil. At one time it was thought that the Lupine caused the poor soil by "wolfing" out the nourishment. Hence, the flower was named after the wolf, which in Latin is *lupus.*

CATTAIL

WHERE FOUND:
Wet places, including ditches, ponds, lake edges and marshes.

FLOWERING SEASON:
May to September.

Cattail Family
Typha latifolia

COMMENTS:
The lower brown flowers, the cattail, are female. Above are the yellowish male flowers which shed their pollen in early summer and leave a bare stem. The lower stem and roots are pure starch and may be eaten raw or toasted. The female flowers may be dried to make excellent tinder.

CATTAIL

INDEX OF COMMON NAMES

INDEX OF SCIENTIFIC NAMES

INDEX BY COLOR

WHITE

THREE PETALS

FOUR PETALS

FIVE PETALS

SIX PETALS

MANY PETALS

RACEME

YELLOW

NO PETALS

TWO PETALS

FOUR PETALS

FIVE PETALS

SIX PETALS

MANY PETALS

RACEME

ORANGE

FOUR PETALS

SIX PETALS

RACEME

RED-PINK

NO PETALS

FOUR PETALS

FIVE PETALS

SIX PETALS

MANY PETALS

RACEME

LAVENDER-PURPLE

THREE PETALS

FOUR PETALS

FIVE PETALS

SIX PETALS

MANY PETALS

RACEME

BLUE

FOUR PETALS

FIVE PETALS

SIX PETALS

MANY PETALS

RACEME

BROWN

RACEME

BIBLIOGRAPHY

Clark, Lewis. *Field Guide, Wild Flowers of Forest & Woodland in the Pacific Northwest.* Sidney, BC, Canada: Gray's Publishing, Ltd., Copyright (c) 1974 by Lewis J. Clark estate.

Craighead, J., Craighead, F. Jr., and Davis, Ray. *A Field Guide to Rocky Mountain Wildflowers.* Boston: Houghton Mifflin Co., 1963.

Dodge, Natt N. *100 Desert Wildflowers.* Tucson, AZ: National Park Service and Southwest Parks & Monuments Association, 1963.

Gilmore, Melvin R. *Uses of Plants by the Indians of the Missouri River Region.* University of Nebraska Press, 1977 (revision of 1914 thesis).

Grimm, William C. *Recognizing Flowering Wild Plants.* Harrisburg, PA: Stackpole Books, 1968.

Inglis, Bessie. *Wild Flower Studies.* New York: The Studio Publications, Inc., with Thomas Y. Crowell Co., 1951.

Kinukan, Edith S., and Brons, Penney R. *Wildflowers of the West.* Ketchum, ID: Kinukan and Brons, 1979.

Lemmon, Robert, and Johnson, Charles C. *Wildflowers of North America.* Garden City, NY: Hanover House, Nelson Doubleday, 1961.

Niehaus, Theodore E., and Ripper, Charles L. *A Field Guide to Pacific States Wildflowers.* The Peterson Field Guide Series ed. Roger Tory Peterson, 1976.

Orr, Robert T., and Orr. Margaret C. *Wildflowers of Western America.* New York: Chanticleer Press Edition, Galahad Books, 1974.

Richard Spellenberg. "Wildflowers." In *Western Forests,* Parts II and II. Chanticleer Press, Alfred Knopf Inc., 1942.

Strickler, Dr. Dee. *Alpine Wildflowers.* Helena, MT: Falcon Press, 1990.

Strickler, Dr. Dee. *Forest Wildflowers.* Columbia Falls, MT: Flower Press, 1988.

Susan J. Wernert, editor. "Wildflowers." *North American Wildlife,* pp. 332-507. Pleasantville, NY: Readers Digest Association, 1982.